THE TRUTH IS REALITY, TWO POINT ZERO

By:

Eileena Warehouser

Website:

www.thetruthisreality20.com

Email:

Thetruthisreality2.0@outlook.com

YouTube: Book Club: The Truth Is Reality; Two Point Zero - YouTube

Audiobooks: www.audiobooks.com/audiobook/truth-is-reality- two-point-zero/611249

TABLE OF CONTENT

TABLE OF CONTENT

PART 1:

RACING TO BE HUMAN

Chapter 1:

SO MANY FOLLOWERS, SO FEW LEADERS

(Note: In this book, you will see many sentences, phrases, thoughts and messages repeated several times. This is intentional. Because we are so thoroughly indoctrinated, saturated and inundated with the follower's way of thinking and the "old" way of doing things ... new ideas, a new awareness, and the process of transitioning philosophies, thoughts, and lifestyle requires repetitive presentation.)

The first step in problem solving is to properly identify the problem. Often, we attempt to solve symptoms of the actual problem. Often, we attempt to or solve related or resulting problems without ever solving the real true problem.

Then we wonder why the problem keeps reoccurring. If you don't get to the root, the genesis, the basis of the problem, by properly identifying the problem, the solutions you choose will not solve the actual problem.

Race issues, office politics, personal relationships, male chauvinism, female catty/petty jealousy issues, and female self-image issues all these items stem from one source: EGO.

Her is a quote from Oprah Winfrey: "Ego is an imposter ..." from her book _The Wisdom of Sundays_.

Although some dictionaries list these words as

synonyms: ego, self-esteem, pride, self-worth, confidence, arrogance, they have very different meanings. Because most people have difficulty differentiating between ego and self-esteem, they never properly identify the problem as being singularly EGO. It disguises itself as self- esteem, pride, ambition, self-worth and confidence, hence the quote: "Ego is an imposter."

Older dictionaries, printed in the 1950s through the 1980s, have defined ego with more psychology academia emphasized definitions, such as the super-ego and "id."

Between two and three years of age, ego's negative vibration or energy attaches to an individual. You've heard of the Terrible Twos. That is when a baby first says: "My name is _____."

They recognize themselves as separate individuals, with their own names and their own possessions such as clothing and toys. They say phrases such as: "These are my clothes." "These are my toys." That's when the Compare & Compete begins. Most parents try to teach their children to be kind, share, and not to bully others. Some children learn these lessons more quickly than others.

Self-esteem should be based on: DOING THE BEST YOU CAN WITH WHAT YOU'VE BEEN GIVEN.

Self-esteem should never be based on Compare & Compete with another person.

It's not an external thing. IT'S AN INTERNAL THING.

The first step in problem solving is: PROPERLY IDENTIFY

THE PROBLEM.

I think of ego as an immature childish, hungry, angry monkey on your back, always wanting attention and always wanting to be fed. The more you feed it, the more it grows. But if you taper off its appetite for attention by not feeding it with attention, complements and flattery, or not letting it feed on other creature's suffering or negative energy, it can go dormant. I don't know if you can ever kill your ego, but you can get it under your control or make it go dormant.

You should learn to recognize ego in yourself and other people. You should know and recognize when your ego is speaking through you or is it really you that is speaking. You can recognize when ego is in control; when you are behaving like a childish brat, "acting out" for attention.

Think about the last time your ego was in control of you. Think about the last time you lost your temper. Think about the last time you got jealous and did something vengeful or hateful. Think about the last time you had to apologize for your words or deeds.

The philosopher Socrates said: "Know thyself." I say: "Know thyself without your ego." Ask yourself: "Who am I without my ego?" Can you make the distinction?

"Ego is an imposter ..." Some people confuse ego with ambition. Ego is not ambition. You can be ambitious without ego. Say these words: "I want to do the best I can with what I've been given. I want to set a goal and aspire to reach it with vigor, enthusiasm, and passion, determined to overcome all obstacles. I want to push myself to my personal best without comparing myself to another person but

11

comparing myself to my previous performance."

Some people use the term "healthy ego." There is such a thing as healthy self-esteem, healthy self-image, healthy self-worth, and healthy net worth. There is NO such thing as healthy ego.

Ego is a sneaky, sly imposter, trying any way it can to get your consent to take control of you either consciously or by default.

A course in Miracles says: (paraphrasing) Every word, action, and deed are either love or a call for love. Meaning: if you treat someone kindly, you are giving live. If you mistreat someone, it is a call for love.

Is that person's behavior a subconscious call for love?

Many people don't even know if or when they are being governed and controlled by their ego.

"Father forgive them for they know not what they do." Luke 23:34

If you do not base your self-esteem on the correct thing, your ego will be eager and happy to deceive you into thinking you should behave in a Compare & Compete, conceited, self- serving manner to boost your self-esteem. But you are not really boosting your self-esteem; you are boosting or feeding your ego. There is a big difference.

Your self-esteem should be based on: doing the best you can with what you've been given. This works best when you are truly and completely honest with yourself. So, you set out to accomplish a goal and at the end, you honestly ask yourself, "Did I put 100% effort into achieving this goal? Did I put adequate time, planning, work, research, and due diligence into reaching this goal? Did I do the best I could with what I was given?" This works in all aspects of your life: home, school, work, the gym, self-care/health, personal relationships, business relationships, and romantic relationships.

I do understand. We are human. We are not perfect. Some days are better than others. Some days we are more energetic than others. Some days we are more motivated than others.

So, if you don't reach your goal, you should be honest, analyze and understand why. It is ok. Don't be too hard on yourself.

BUT DO BE COMPLETELY HONEST WITH YOURSELF and try to do better next time.

Don't do the Compare & Compete unless you compare yourself to yourself and how you did previously, trying to attain your personal best.

Whenever I hear someone say, "I am very competitive" I translate that to mean, "I am a very egotistical person."

There are all kinds of competitive events {sports, athletic, academic, music, fashion}. Depending on your level of spiritual awakening and maturity, you may now re-evaluate if you continue to watch these events or how you choose to respond to these events. Can you recognize the contestant's/participant's egos? bragging, taunting, talking shit. Can you recognize your ego? bragging, taunting, talking shit. If you have your self-esteem based on the right thing, an opponent talking shit to you, it won't throw you off your game.

We view these events as a normal part of life and normal part of our culture. But this is the "Follower" mentality. This is another way the ego is an imposter posing as an acceptable part of our lives and culture.

CAUTION!!! Be very careful to keep your ego out of your entertainment and recreation. You have gone too far when you experience anger, frustration, cursing, crying. If you are emotional about it, you have gone too far. If you are betting money on it, you have gone too far.

You can let your children participate in competitions but teach them not to let a win feed their egos. Learning to work within a team is important. Learning to do your personal best and to give 100% effort is important. You can set a goal to win and boost your self-esteem because you have done the best you could with what you were given.

You can compare your current accomplishments with your previous performance to analyze where to improve to achieve your personal best. Earning academic and athletic scholarships are a great thing and provide great opportunities.

[Note: there is a chapter in this book titled: College is for Everyone. We can all have a Piece of the Pie]

Keep your ego out of your goals. If you or your child wants to play sports in a professional league, what is the reason? For the money and fame? Or to push yourself to perform [not compete] on your personal highest level?

Remember, money to provide for your needs, your safety, and living a well-rounded life (with travel, vacations, hobbies, entertainment, fun stuff and recreation) can attained through working hard in college, grad school and earning an honest living and mastering the law of attraction. Your desire for money should not be for fame, bragging, boasting, showing off, or specially not for the Compare & Compete. Those are all ego driven motives.

"The ego is an imposter."

In older dictionaries, from the 1980s and older, it is unlikely you will find the definition of ego to include words such as personality, self-esteem, and self-worth. Back then, they tended to use definitions from the psychology and psychiatry academia [super-ego, id]. The ego wants to deceive you into thinking it is you and an inseparable part of your personality. The ego wants you to believe it is a part of oneself, having the dictionaries list synonyms with the word self, such as self-esteem and self-worth.

You are a soul, a spiritual being, having a temporary human experience. You know your body is temporary. We cry at burials when we place a loved one's temporary shell/body into the ground. More people are now using the phrase, "They made their transition." The soul transitioned out of the body. The soul exits the body.

The ego (a negative energy field/force) attaches itself to your temporary body between two and three years of age.

YOUR EGO IS NOT YOU!

But if you do not realize that fact, your ego will deceive you into thinking it is you and part of your personality. Ego is an imposter, pretending to be you. If you FEED your ego or allow your ego to be fed by complements, flattery, and attention; your ego will keep growing. If you FEED your ego by disrespecting and degrading others; your ego will continue to grow. If you FEED your ego by bragging, boasting; your ego will grow even more. If you keep feeding your ego, it will become fat, overweight, overbearing,

and take you over. If you are not educated on the facts of who and what your ego really is, you won't know the difference between you and your ego.

You have heard people say, "My ego was out of control" or "My ego got the best of me." You may have even said these words yourself while apologizing for some hurtful thing you did to someone else.

I am not saying don't accept complements. Use good manners and common courtesy, smile and say thank you, when receiving a complement.

Here is a question for you: Do you know the difference between a complement and flattery?

{Note: there is a chapter in this book about "Other people's opinions." Your self-esteem should not be based on other people's opinions: good or bad. We will elaborate on that topic in that chapter.}

Some schools of thought say we all need to do shadow work, that we all have a dark side, and we need to let it out from time to time or let it out in a controlled or constructive manner.

I think the dark side is ego, and ego is an imposter. Ego wants you to believe it is you or part of the spectrum of you.

I'll repeat it like this: you are a DIVINE spiritual being having a temporary human experience in a temporary human body. You are not your ego. You are a spiritual being having a temporary human experience.

Put these two common thoughts and phrases together: "Your body is the temple of God" and "God is Love."

If _____, then _____.

If your body is the temple of God and God is Love, then you are _____! (fill in the blank) Your body is the temple of Love. You are Love. {incarnate}

Shadow work can be constructive and therapeutic for some people. But try this, stop feeding your ego. Stop growing your ego. Understand, your ego is not you. Your self-esteem should be based on doing the best you can with what you've been given, not Compare & Compete.

Bad, evil thoughts and ideas come from being on a low vibration and low frequency. Like a radio frequency, wherever you tune your dial, you will receive the broadcast disseminated on that frequency.

Do a web search for: Vibrational Frequency Chart

If you are living, wallowing, and dwelling in a low-frequency range, most of the time (the majority of your day is spent on a low frequency), low-frequency thoughts, ideas, and circumstances will be attracted to you and enter your life. Your ego will be glad to suggest what to do with those bad, evil thoughts and ideas, most likely, something to feed or boost your ego.

Do you think you create your thoughts and ideas? I'm talking about original thoughts, not a memory, not a conclusion from study and analysis. Original thoughts. Original ideas.

Suppose you are living, loving, and dwelling in happiness and positivity, on higher frequency emotions. In that case, you will receive thoughts and ideas, from the universe, of a higher frequency and positive nature.

Do you watch horror movies? Are the scenes darkly lit [low frequency]? Was the music created and played on a low frequency? Is the music evoking low frequency emotions? Are you putting gross and gruesome images into your memory?

Do you listen to music where they are bragging, boasting, showing off, degrading and battling others? Ever listen to hip-hop? What is that going to do to your ego and frequency after listening to that all day?

{Note: there is a chapter in this book asking: Is hip-hop really art? We will elaborate on that topic in that chapter}

The ego is an imposter. The ego wants you to think shadow work is beneficial. How can intentionally putting yourself on a low frequency be a good thing? You think you are bringing up and working through bad feelings, destructive emotions or past traumatic events, but remember, for the most part, in most situations, your ego fed you the negativity, darkness and low frequency in the first place. Ego is like, "Come on into this shadow work center, and let me reiterate and reinforce these low-frequency emotions like guilt, anger, and shame, among others, and let me help you recall and wallow in bad memories for a few days."

The first step in problem solving is properly identifying the problem.

Shadow work is fine if you correctly identify the problem. I wholeheartedly believe shadow workers have good intentions. You've heard the saying, "The read to hell is paved with good intentions." In some cases, shadow work may yield good results permanently, and in other cases, the results may be very temporary.

Just know that your ego is not you. You are a divine soul having a temporary human experience in a temporary human body. Ego and self-esteem two very different words, items, and concepts.

Now that you are in the process of learning more and knowing more, you will behave in a more mature and enlightened manner. When you know better, you do better. Before reading this book, you used to be governed and controlled by your ego. In your past, you used to base your self-esteem on compare and compete. Before reading this book, (chapter 10) you used to base your self-esteem on other people's opinions.

You used to be thin skinned and defensive, hiding behind your ego's defense mechanisms. Before reading this book, you used to run your ambition on ego, using other people, stepping on and backstabbing to get ahead in your goals. After reading to this book, you know there is a big difference between ego and self-esteem. After reading this book, you know the correct basis on which your self-esteem should be created and grown.

Self-esteem should be based on doing the best you can with what you've been given, not on Compare & Compete.

Don't feel guilt or shame about your past because when you know better, you do better.

Most people (80% of the world's population) are followers, as opposed to Leaders (10% of the population) or individuals (10% of the population). This is demonstrated by the fact that 90% of the world's wealth is owned by 1% of the population. That 1% is made up of leaders and individuals.

Some schools of thought agree that most humans only use 10% of their brain's capability during their lifetime. Now some of you will scoff at that statement, "Most people only use 10% of their brain's capability during their lifetime," saying this statement has been proven to be erroneous.

Well, I say, you must pay attention to details. I did NOT say: most people only use 10% of their brain's capacity during their lifetime.

Definitions:

Capacity: the maximum amount something can contain.

Capability: the power or ability to do something.

Just as you can train, practice, and use your body to perform extraordinary athletic accomplishments, such as running a marathon, you can train, practice, and use your brain to achieve extraordinary intellectual accomplishments.

You definitely can increase your brain's CAPABILITY.

There is always more to know, and there is always room to grow. Knowledge is infinite. Your ego wants you to be arrogant and smug and ASSUME you know more than the next person, always looking to see if you are the smartest person in the room, or the wealthiest person in the room. Stay humble and always be willing to listen. Always be willing to learn more, no matter the source.

You and I know we can accomplish a great deal more than what we are currently doing. The most crucial step is to believe you can achieve whatever goal you have set for yourself.

Followers follow the crowd. Followers follow what is most popular. Followers want to feel as if they are part of the crowd. They are uncomfortable standing alone. They have to have someone else agree with them. They can't make a decision by themselves. They always have to ask someone else's opinion or follow and imitate what they see others do.

It is wise to seek counsel when it is available. Problem-solving skills and decision-making skills should be developed and mastered in each individual.

If someone comes along who is different from the crowd and is not trying to be a part of the crowd (not a follower), a comparison is made attempting to separate and determine who is right and who is wrong, who is better and who is worse. Most followers can't comprehend, understand, and accept that some people are just simply different, not right or wrong, not better or worse … just simply different.

Followers don't like when they meet someone different from the crowd. Followers don't like people who are not trying to be like the crowd, not trying to blend in with the crowd. Followers do not like independent individuals. They feel awkward, uncomfortable, and insecure around independent individuals. People fear what they don't understand, and they hate what they fear. Followers DO like leaders, so they can be lazy, follow the leader, and let go of being responsible and thinking independently.

Not all independent individuals want to be or need to be leaders. Leaders like followers. Often, it is an ego trip for a leader to have followers. Most of the time, independent individuals don't mind helping others by taking a leadership role. Independent individuals innately have leadership skills, qualities and characteristics. But at some point, the autonomous individual will expect the follower to step up and go their separate way.

The FOLLOWER and the EGO:

The followers erroneously follow the popular opinion that self-esteem should be based on material possessions and physical appearance. It is called the "EGO BONUS POINT SYSTEM." They constantly compare themselves to whomever they encounter, trying to see how they stack up against the next person. They compare their cars, houses, clothes, and any other material possessions they have. They also compare their physical appearance.

When the comparison is made, if the Follower feels they have the better in the comparison, they EARN an ego bonus point. If they do not have the better in the comparison, they lose an ego bonus point.

If they lose an ego bonus point, they do shallow, superficial acts (sometimes vengeful, hateful, and hurtful acts) to earn the ego bonus point back. Examples of these acts are: talking/gossiping badly about the other person or being mean to the other person, or being mean to whomever they encounter, taking their frustrations out wherever possible.

The current popular term/slang is called: "Hater."

Self-esteem should be based on doing the best you can with what you've been given.

Some people have the privilege of being born into wealthy families. Some people are born into poverty. Some people experience traumatic and tragic circumstances, which set them back.
Some people have the appearance of wealth but are up to their eyeballs in debt. Some obtain wealth illegally and will soon lose their wealth.

There are thousands of success stories of people who made it out of poverty through education and hard work through legal means. The key is to BELIEVE that you can do it. Stop following the crowd straight to hell. Don't let unfortunate circumstances and obstacles hold you back. Stop wasting time following people on the gram, Facebook, and other social media platforms or following what's trending and trying to stay on trend.

{Note: later in this book, we will discuss smartphones, tablets, iPad, computers, and how the size of your ego is directly proportionate to your screentime.}

When doing the best you can with what you've been given, you have to be completely honest with yourself about doing your absolute very best, because in your private moments when you have to face yourself, when you have to face the truth and reality. You may have to admit to yourself, "Damn, I really could have done more" or "I really could have put more time into that" or "I know I held back for selfish reasons." If you know you did not do your very best, your self-esteem will fall drastically, and you may not know the right way to pick yourself back up.

Take advantage of every educational opportunity. If your job offers tuition reimbursement/tuition assistance or additional training, take advantage of that. If your job provides fitness club memberships or membership discounts, take advantage of that. As opportunities present themselves, you should take advantage of them. This is a big part of doing the best you can with what you've been given.

The Compare & Compete should never be done or even contribute to determining one's self- worth. Your self-esteem should not be based on material possessions. Unless you are Jeff Bezos, there will always be someone with better/more material possessions than you. The Compare & Compete should not be done in the first place.

Keeping up with the Joneses and Ego Bonus Points leads to petty jealousy, envy, and negativity. Keeping up with the Joneses can become a vicious, dangerous cycle escalating into living beyond your means, putting yourself, your credit, and your family at risk. Festering negative thoughts, jealousy, and anger attracts negative energy and attracts more negative circumstances into your life.

{Note: there is a chapter in this book discussing how to overcome jealousy}

The Compare & Compete should not be done because

your soul's journey through _this lifetime_ is very different from any other soul's (person's) journey during _this lifetime_. During this lifetime, the life lessons you are to learn are very different from another person's life lessons. A soul born into wealth has other lessons to learn to learn during this lifetime than a soul born into poverty.

You don't know what stage another soul is in – on their journey, how many incarnations, how many lifetimes have occurred, what lessons they still have to learn, what lessons you still have to learn, therefore do not Compare & Compete.

You are comparing apples and oranges. Stay on your path. Stay in your lane. You are an immortal divine soul having a temporary human

experience in a temporary human body. Your body is the temple of God. God is Love. You are Love incarnate. You are not your ego. You are not evil.

People say, "that is human nature." Evil is not human nature. Greed is not human nature. Evil is EGO NATURE. Greed is EGO NATURE. Selfishness is EGO NATURE. Narcissism is EGO NATURE.

You don't have to believe in reincarnation to grasp this concept. Suppose you believe you will go to heaven or hell after this lifetime. In that case, you also believe you have certain lessons to learn and specific behaviors, virtues, and accomplishments to achieve before you make it to heaven or hell. And these differ from person to person. So don't Compare & Compete, because your requirements for heaven or hell may be different from the next person's. Your strengths and weaknesses may be very different from the next person's.

Unfortunately, some people (controlled by ego) thrive on negativity. Unfortunately, some people need to degrade others to make themselves feel better about themselves [gain ego bonus points].

Sarcasm, smart remarks, jabs, and zings are indicators of an inflated ego. This ego is attempting to create hurtful, negative feelings in someone else. It indicates that the individual doesn't feel good about themself, trying to bring another person down.

Psychology professionals call this "Leveling" – searching for reasons or making statements to degrade others to bring them down to what you genuinely perceive as your level or lower.

****

Use it or lose it. Use more of your brain capability or lose it. Many adults go back to school after taking a break, sometimes a very long break. Often, they say they have to get back into the habit of studying. If you learn and practice problem-solving skills, your brain will maintain and sharpen your ability to solve problems. If you learn and practice decision- making skills, your brain will maintain and sharpen your ability to make good decisions.

Many people take review courses and then take the BAR or the CPA exam and pass on their first try. Many people train for a minimum of six months and then run marathons (26.2 miles). Most people don't even push for or explore their full potential.

Most people only aspire to have mundane or ordinary lifestyles because it is all they see their peers and family members achieve. They are followers. The American Dream (western culture) is to own a house and a car. Followers believe if you own a home and a car, you are doing well.

Some people think it is noble, virtuous, and admirable only to have humble aspirations. They say things like, "I'm not trying to be rich," or "I'm not asking for much," or "I just want to be able to pay my bills." Some people are taught that rich people are bad, mean and greedy. Well, some are and some are not.

But an individual who does not push themselves to achieve their full potential is cheating themselves and the rest of the world out of their God-given talents and gifts. You were given a BILLION-DOLLAR BRAIN. Why are you only using $50,000 of it? If someone gave you a check for a BILLION dollars, would you only accept $50,000 of it, and refuse the rest, then say, "I'm being noble, virtuous, and humble?"

You owe prosperity to your family. You owe prosperity to the world. Someone is sitting on the cure for cancer because they are not pushing themselves to their full potential. Someone is sitting on the solution for global warming because they are not pushing themselves to their full potential. Someone is sitting on the solution for world hunger because they are not pushing themselves to their full potential. Someone is sitting on the resolution for world peace because they are not pushing themselves to their full potential. Is this you?

Becoming rich does not have to be your primary motive, and you don't have to keep all of your monetary gain s for yourself. You can always donate to a worthy charity. It is not noble or admirable to cheat the world out of your God-given talents and gifts.

The brain craves stimulation and growth. Most people only use 10% of their brain's capability during a lifetime. If an individual does not consciously find positive, progressive activities to stimulate their mind and body, thy will subconsciously or by default direct their energy into negative destructive activities. These activities include criminal, deviant, mean, and vengeful activities.

A popular football star experienced legal difficulties because of his involvement with an illegal dog-fighting ring. He, his family, and his friends who ran this organization could have put their energy and resources into completing their formal educations, and setting up and operating legal, positive, productive enterprises.

There is a famous hip-hop artist who started a youth football league. Many celebrities use their wealth to fund youth mentoring programs, sports leagues, and education programs.

Use your powers for good. It will come back to you. You will reap what you sow.

When having an intelligent conversation, your opinions should be based on facts. If your opinions are based on fabrication, your opinion will not hold much validity, and therefore it is not an intelligent conversation.

If Peyton Manning had been busted for running a

dogfighting ring, some people say that he would have received a much lighter sentence. This statement is not factual. This statement is complete fabrication. Because Peyton Manning

has never been convicted of operating a dogfighting ring, we do not – IN FACT – know what type of sentence he would have received.

When having an intelligent conversation, why fabricate statements that only create negative emotions and negative energy. This festering and wallowing in negativity only attracts more negative circumstances.

When having an intelligent conversation, try to stick with the facts.

Here are some facts:

The FACT is, if you choose to break the law, YOU will face consequences. If you are convicted, the punishment can range from time served, fines, community service, probation, one day and up to life imprisonment. It really doesn't matter what someone else could have, could have, or would have received as punishment for a crime.

In their dubiously intelligent conversations, the followers, with their follower mentality, often start sentences with "he probably …" [" he prolly"],   … then finish the sentence with some negative and non-factual statement. This is a weak way to sound (on the surface) as though you have some support information to validate your opinion. When *IN FACT,* it is pure fabrication and speculation.

Have you ever taken a statistic class? Do you know how to calculate a probability?

Keep it real.

The truth is sometimes embarrassing and hurtful.

People often say that Caucasian athletes would receive lighter sentences than African American athletes if convicted of the same crimes.

I do recognize and acknowledge that racial injustice exists in the world. My point is: if you break the law, there are consequences, so stop breaking the law.

When given the rare opportunity, privilege, and honor to participate in professional sports, why would you risk losing that over some stupid shit?

THE TRUTH

Another reason we keep repeating the same errors and keep missing the mark in solving the real true problem is that people choose not to - or- simply refuse to recognize "THE TRUTH."

Because most people are Followers, they adopt popular opinions, beliefs, traditions, and what's trending. They follow the crowd. They are too lazy to do their research and analysis to formulate their own opinion for their own reasons.

"The Truth" and "A Lie" were walking down the road to a small village. Along the way, they came to a lake of water. "A Lie" suggested that they jump in and take a swim. After some talking and convincing, "The Truth" finally agreed to take a swim. So, "The Truth" took off its clothes and jumped into the lake of water.

While the truth was under the water, "A Lie" put on "The Truth's" clothes and ran to the village spreading lies all around. The people in the village believed "A Lie" because he was clothed in the "Robe of Truth."

When "The Truth" finally got out of the lake and ran to the village spreading "The Truth," no one would believe him because ... THEY COULDN'T HANDLE THE NAKED TRUTH!!!

Most people can't handle The Naked Truth. Some people like to manipulate The Truth to serve their own purposes. Some people like to sugarcoat The Truth. Some people like to exaggerate The Truth. Some people simply ignore The Truth and live in denial. Some people like to suppress The Truth and pretend it doesn't exist.

The Truth manipulated in any form or fashion is no longer the truth.

A person's sanity is directly proportionate with their ability to comprehend and accept The Truth.

If you are a habitual, compulsive liar or putting on a front pretending that you are something that you genuinely are not, or you have convinced yourself that you are something that you are not, then you do not have a firm grip on reality.

The Truth and Reality will confront you sooner or later, periodically, occasionally or often. You can count on that.

Do you have a firm grip on reality, or are you living a lie? Are you trying to outrun The Truth, thinking it won't catch up with you?

Some people over emphasize positivity. They want to sugarcoat reality. I agree that we should be optimistic and hope for the best, but you must be realistic and always have a contingency plan (a backup plan) just in case things don't go your way.

The human mind is more powerful than most people realize. Remember most people only use 10% of their brain's capability during their lifetime. THERE IS POWER IN POSITIVE THINKING.

Most people are afraid to be truthful at all times because they don't want to hurt another person's feelings. But the fact is, The Truth is not always a pleasant thing. The Truth is sometimes painful, brutal, or embarrassing. It CAN be delivered in a more tactful manner. Just make sure your intention is NOT to hurt or belittle someone.

Your intention should be to help. I am NOT saying sugarcoat The Truth. If you have to deliver some harsh or embarrassing truth, take that person to a private place and start by saying, "I am about to tell you something that may hurt you, but hurting you is not my intention. My intention is to help you. This is something you need to know."

CHAPTER TWO: BASIC BLACK AND WHITE DON'T JUST "TOLERATE" ME; UNDERSTAND ME

(Note: In this book, you will see many sentences, phrases, thoughts and messages repeated several times. This is intentional. Because we are so thoroughly indoctrinated, saturated and inundated with the follower's way of thinking and the "old" way of doing things; ... new ideas, a new awareness, and the process of transitioning philosophies, thoughts, and lifestyle requires repetitive presentation.)

"People fear what they don't understand, and people hate what they fear." Don't just tolerate me; understand me.

To me, the word tolerance implies a certain degree of impatience and discomfort, as if deep down inside you are saying, "I honestly dislike you, but I will use my self-discipline, restraint, and maturity to cover up my true feelings so we can - painstakingly- get through this co-existence, together."

PROPERLY IDENTIFY THE PROBLEM

Followers follow the crowd. Followers want to feel like they are a part of the crowd. If they encounter someone else who is different from the crowd and is not even making an effort to be the same as the crowd, a comparison is made to separate and determine who is right or wrong, better or worse. Most followers can't comprehend, understand, and accept that some people/things are simply different, not right or wrong, better or worse, just simply: different.

Racism comes from EGO. Some people have the erroneous need to degrade others to make themselves feel better about themselves.

It may not be time permitting, or the situation may not be conducive to familiarizing yourself with someone else's heritage, history, or culture. But it is obvious, there are differences. The ego wants to compare and compete, then rank everyone in degrees of better and worse. There are good people and bad people in every race. Start everyone on an even playing field and deal with each person on an individual basis.

There is an unquestionable comfort level when we are amongst our own, and people feel ok with stereotyping, generalizing, and using racial slurs. In these situations, the follower mentality is in abundance. People are hesitant or afraid to speak up and say: "I am offended, and I disagree with that racial slur. I don't lump all of that race into one category."

Ego, materialism, greed, and the follower mentality (everyone follows the SAME lifestyle and Christianity or you are wrong) motivated and drove the Europeans to become explorers [colonizers]. They set out to find and steal treasures from other lands. They would simply label the natives as heathens and sub-human in their erroneous attempt to justify raping, pillaging, thieving, and stripping the natural resources from other lands.

35

The Europeans labeled themselves as good and the Africans or other natives, from other lands, as evil. And they would even take the land and call it "colonization." They called it colonization, the spread of civilization, and Christian missionary work. Still, the truth and reality is that they were raping, pillaging, thieving, and stripping resources from other lands. They manipulated lies and disguised them as "THE TRUTH" to justify their brutal and horrifying behavior.

The conqueror gets to write or re-write HIS- story to say whatever he chooses. The conqueror gets to write or re-write HIS - story to omit whatever he chooses, as well.

****

Why did the colonizers call the Africans uncivilized heathens?

Source: Bondy Blue's YouTube Channel: "BBS Oprah Interviews Meghan Markle"

The African's appearance, dress style, shelter, and infrastructure were very different from the Europeans.

Everyone looks the way they look and lives the way they live because of their geographical location on the planet. It doesn't mean one group is more civilized than the other.

If you live in a building and wear clothing, it

36

doesn't make you more civilized. It means you live in a location where the climate necessitates living in a building with windows and doors to shut out and seal out the cold.

Back in the colonial days, the Africans lived in a hut and wore little to no clothing, because they lived in extremely hot, tropical climates.

They didn't have A/C back when the colonizers first raped Africa, not the second time either, but maybe by the sixth or seventh time, but definitely by the twentieth time.

An individual's nostrils may be larger because they need more filtration while breathing in more hot, humid air and they need enough oxygen to fuel dense, strong muscles.
An individual's nostrils may be small because they live in a colder climate, with thin air, and/or at higher altitudes.

****

Please view: Chimamanda Adichie Speech at the Humboldt Forum - YouTube

****

The main reason the colonizers adopted and facilitated slavery of Africans was to build and work on the plantations in the hot climate of the southern states, and the Caribbean. The colonizers themselves couldn't handle working in the hot sun. The colonizers had no right to kidnap, maim, beat, torture, rape, murder, enslave, and never pay the Africans for their labor.

Human beings are different from other animals because of the capability to communicate, use reasoning and logic to resolve issues, and the ability to build shelter and infrastructure on an advanced level. Civilized humans should use their intellect to problem-solve instead of using violence, weapons and physical overpowering another human being.

The true history of the many dynasties, nations, leaders, and cultures from the continent of Africa has been hidden, suppressed and deleted as opposed to the widespread dissemination and inclusion as classroom educational material of European history.

Most white people and many African Americans think Africans living on the continent of Africa are now and have always been uneducated, primitive, uncivilized jungle bunnies. They credit white men and colonization for bringing technology and formal education to advance the continent.

Most people don't know that ancient Egypt (Greek name)/Kemet (African name) (black people, not Arabs) were the most advanced civilization on the planet during their heyday. The Greeks and Romans attended the Mystery Schools in Kemet. Many other countries on the African continent were more technologically advanced than the rest of the world. (Atlantis was in the Eye of the Sahara)

Because of ego, the Greeks, Romans, Europeans, and Arabs (commissioned by the white man) went to Africa and stripped, robbed, raped, stole, enslaved, disrupted and corrupted most of the northern continent. Arabs enslaved more Africans than the white man.

Research Shaka Zulu. Research how by damming (building barriers to disrupt the flow) the Nile River has caused famine in parts of the continent. Research blood diamonds. Research the true cause and reason for the Somali pirates. Read these books: 1. *Stolen Legacy* by: George J.M. James 2. *They Came Before Columbus* by Ivan Van Sertima 3. *The African Origin of Civilization: Myth or Reality* by: Cheikh Anta Diop 4. *The Destruction of Black Civilization: Great Issues of a Race from 4500 B.C. to 2000 A.D* by: Chancellor Williams

White supremacists think they are superior because they are the ruling class in Europe and most of North America (not including Mexico). But you need to consider how they became the ruling class; by robbing, raping, enslaving, stealing, killing, violating universal laws, crimes against nature and crimes against humanity. Why would you be proud of that? They try to make themselves seem ethically and morally superior when they are the perpetrators of the most insidious, despicable, heinous, disgusting, reprehensible, abhorrent, horrifying, un-scrupulous, villainous crimes and genocides on this planet. Why would you be proud of that?

Why would a person be proud of the losing side (The Confederacy) of the U.S. Civil War? Why would a person be proud of the Confederate flag?

Some people try to say the confederate flag does not represent the desire for slavery. To those people, I say, please read the 1861 Corner stone speech by Alexander Stephens. Read the *Ordinance of Succession*. Why would you be proud of heritage and ancestors who have taught hate and ignorance, passing it down from one generation to the next generation and the next?

White supremacists think they are superior because they are the ruling class of the 750 million population of Europe, the 360 million population of the United States and Canada, Iceland and Greenland. Are white people the ruling class of the 365 million population in South America? No. Are white people the ruling class of the 4.5 billion population of

Asia? No. What color are the indigenous people of India? Are white people the ruling class of the 1.3 billion population of the continent of Africa? No. What color are the indigenous people of Australia? The population of Australia is 40 million. You do the math.

What made the European explorers/colonizers feel they had the right to invade and occupy other people's property [O.P.P.]? Answer: Ego.

George Santayana said, "Those who do not remember the past are condemned to repeat it." Why did Vladimir Putin feel he could invade Ukraine? Answer: Ego

They said it is the natural order of things, and the white man is superior to the black man. They said it is survival of the fittest. This phrase accurately refers to animals of a lower family, genus and species. That is why we say treat people with humanity and in a humane manner. Do not treat other people in an atrocious, inhumane way. Do not condone inhumane living conditions.

If you are human, you are able to read and comprehend what is written on the pages of this book. If you put this book in front of any other species, they cannot read or comprehend the sentences printed on the pages of this book. We are rightfully held to a higher standard than other animals. The some "natives" and indigenous people on many continent and islands lived in harmony with nature and the planet. Most were spiritual, had regard, respect, and reverence for human life and all life. Most were compassionate and forgiving. It was not their core precepts and code of conduct/ethics to kill mercilessly and needlessly or steal or take what did not rightfully belong to them or what they did not earn. It is for these very reasons that some natives were able to be conquered. some natives didn't fight and kill on offense. Fighting and killing on defense was done with hesitation and anguish.

The systems are in place worldwide to sabotage and stunt the psyche, education and self-esteem of all darker melanated people.

Dear Black People,

Despite the systematic and institutionalized oppression of our people, please don't be angry and go through life with a chip on your shoulder. Being negative and functioning/living within a low vibrational range will attract adverse and low vibration circumstances into your life. Your ego wants you to be angry and resentful. Your ego wants you to do the compare & compete.

Here is what you should do: look in the mirror and say: "My creator blessed me with this beautiful melanin rich body and beautiful brown or black skin to journey through **_THIS life-time_**, to learn certain lessons and accomplish what is required for my soul to ascend to the next level." Use positivity and the law of attraction to obtain what you want and need in this life.

If you wallow, fester, and dwell on negative thoughts, anger and resentment, you will attract negativity into your life. Take the high road, despite the covert and overt racism. Rise above it all. Guard your peace. Guard your vibration and frequency. Even though we want to support African American film-makers, actors, and entertainers, if you experience negative emotions, sadness, or anger when watching the news, civil rights news clips, slavery, civil rights documentaries and movies, police brutality news clips or other informational sources, you need to avoid them. I am not saying, "Don't be informed and educated on these topics." Yes, do be informed and educated on these topics, but don't wallow, fester, and stew in the negativity of these topics. Guard your peace. Guard your positive energy. Guard your vibration and frequency.

Sincerely, your sistah, Eileena

From where does the "B" in the R&B music come? What happens to you if you listen to the Blues for an extended amount of time?

Racism continues to exist. The fact is there are good people and bad people in every race. Which are you? There are highly intelligent and highly unintelligent people in every race. Which are you? You should approach and interact with people on an individual basis.

Even if you are forewarned that someone is a racist (for example, in a work environment), proceed with caution but still interact with that person on an individual basis. In a work environment, make an extra effort to remain professional and mature. Document and make copies of these documents of behavior that is racist toward you.

Don't be paranoid. Keep your mind clear and sharp, so you can detect if someone's racism is systematically trying to harm you, bring you down, or get you fired. Stay away from mind- altering drugs, especially in the workplace, so that you can be clear, alert, and as aware as possible.

If you are threatened with violence, and you are in a defensive situation (not offensive) where you need to defend your life, your family or your friend's life, then do so within the limits of the law.

Name-calling, racial slurs, and racist jokes should be overlooked. Your self-esteem and self-worth should not be based on someone else's opinion. You can be above that immature mentality. The follower mentality tells you to react with anger and violence when someone calls you a name, degrades you or attempts to insult you. Mature, confident individuals are not adversely affected by immature taunting or being called a nigger.

Unfortunately, some people thrive on negativity. Unfortunately, some people need to degrade others to make themselves feel better about themselves (gain EGO BONUS POINTS).

Sarcasm, smart remarks, jabs, zings are indicators of a sick ego. This sick ego is attempting to create hurtful, negative feelings in someone else. It indicates that the individual doesn't truly feel good about themselves.

Psychology professionals call this "Leveling," searching for reasons or making statements to degrade others to bring them down to what they perceive is their level or below.

An African American teenager was expelled from school for beating up a white classmate for calling him a nigger.

Please don't get caught in this trap, and IT IS A TRAP! Teach your children not to get caught in this trap. It will take a lot of strength and maturity, but don't lose your composure over some juvenile name calling. IT IS NOT WORTH IT. Your self- esteem and self-worth should not be based on the opinion of the name-caller or the bystanders (instigators) who hear the name-calling.

"Success is 10% of what happens to you and 90% of how you react to it."

"Stick and stones may break my bones, but names will never hurt me." Names **should never** hurt you. **Names can only hurt you; IF YOU LET THEM!**

The immature follower mentality tells you to react with anger and violence when a non-black call you a nigger. I do not care if a white person calls me a nigger. I smile and say, "I'll pray for you." My self-esteem and self-worth are not even the tiniest fractions, based on their opinion of me. Using such a slur is a significant indicator of an ignorant individual. It is more likely they don't know me or know anything about me, so why would I care if they "think" they are superior to me or want to degrade me with a racial slur. They want me to fall into their TRAP, sink to their level. They want to steal my joy. They want to steal my peace. They want me to think negative thoughts and attract negativity into my life.

Yes, in the big picture, it is that deep. The enslavement of Africans was to steal their power (physical and mental power), to steal their power of positive thinking, steal their magic, disconnect them from their language and their ancestors, disconnect them from their collective intelligence and history, and most of all disconnect them from their most powerful spirituality and forcing watered down [white- washed] religion on them.

The Imus event, the Jena 6 event …

One possible reaction statement would be:

"I hope you take the time to do some soul searching to deter- mine why you feel the need to degrade others with name calling. If there are facts to support your criticism, I am open to discuss constructive criticism for my ultimate betterment. If your motive is to make me feel bad, degrade me or embarrass me, I must inform you that my self-esteem is not, in the least bit, or in the smallest fraction, based on your opinion. Unfortunately, some people thrive on negativity. Unfortunately, some people have the twisted need to degrade others to make themselves feel better about themselves." (gain EGO BONUS POINTS). Sarcasm, smart remarks, jabs, and zings are indicators of sick egos. This sick ego is attempting to create hurtful, negative feelings in someone else. It indicates that the individual doesn't truly feel good about themselves."

Dr. Martin Luther King, Jr. led non-violent protests for equal civil rights. Why did they work? The protests worked because they showed that African Americans could be intelligent, mature, civilized and deserve the right to live, work, and be educated in humane conditions. It took a great deal of maturity and determination for the demonstrators * NOT* to react to the name-calling, taunting and violence brought against them.

In U.S. history, part of the (FALSE) justification for slavery was they said the slaves were incapable of learning to read & write. That reasoning has obviously been proven wrong. Then, they made it illegal to teach the slaves to read & write because KNOWLEDGE IS POWER! Knowledge plus action is power.

Don't sink to the level of the name caller. Don't give them an excuse. Don't fall into their trap. Once you get your self-esteem and self-worth based on the right thing (not based on anything **external**: such as name-calling, other people's opinions), you will not lose your temper over insignificant external items.

Dear White People: being pro-black and "Black Lives Matter" does not mean anti-white. Sincerely, Eileena

I am quite happy and pleased with the human body my creator gave me, the beautiful natural melanin sunscreen cocoa brown skin, and my naturally curly, wavy hair. I assure you; it is very soft. Take my word for it. You are not welcome to touch it. You just want to compare and compete. You just want to see if you have another reason to degrade me.

When I see people [most often white women, some Asians] excessively flipping their hair, I wonder, are they trying to make me jealous? I am not jealous. My inclination is that this person has an ego imbalance. I can use this to my advantage by complimenting her, stroking her ego, dumbing down my behavior and vocabulary, getting her to drop her guard or under- estimate me, then I will use the strategic advantage of the element of surprise.

My point is that I recognize certain behaviors in an attempt to cause me to have negative feelings,   … which I reject.

Some egos CAN NOT escape the compare and compete and the need to categorize everything and every situation as a "W" or an "L."   … the properly identified problem.

****

Don't be a racist. The fact is there are good people and bad people in every race. Which are you? There are highly intelligent and highly unintelligent people in every race. Which are you? You should approach and interact with people on an individual basis. There are trustworthy and untrustworthy people in every race.

You know the red flags, you know when you have a gut feeling, but search for facts to support your gut feelings.

You may be missing out on a life-long loyal friendship, a highly profitable rewarding business opportunity, or the love of your life simply because you excluded someone because of the color of their skin.

POLICE BRUTALITY AND EXCESSIVE FORCE

Properly Identify the Problem EGO.

Many have suggested solutions that will undoubtedly make a big difference, such as stringent vetting, background checks, verifying work history, verifying references, not re-hiring formerly terminated police officers, psychological

analysis, personality testing, diversity training, terminating, prosecuting and convicting the users of excessive force and terminating, prosecuting and convicting police officers who are murderers.

I have heard people say many police officers are people who were bullied in high school, they have carried a chip on their shoulders, and as police officers, they have the means to carry out authority fantasies.

The creation of the police force in the United States is rooted in racism. Many of the original law enforcement units, in the south, started with the slave patrol.

Please

view:

The Evolution of Law Enforcement – YouTube

The Racist Origins of U.S. Law – YouTube

Why Do We Have Private Prisons? – YouTube

Who Makes Money From Private Prisons? – YouTube

If a person does not know the difference between

self-esteem and ego, they will abuse their authority and power if their ego is in control of them.

The term: defunding the police is problematic. I humbly suggest the terms: "down-sizing" or "right sizing." (throw back to the 1980s and 1990s.) We have to deconstruct the old, then start over, creating an entirely new police force.

Please read: *The Color of Law; A forgotten History of How Our Government Segregated America* by Mr. Richard Rothstein

****

The following is taken from, *The Daily Show* June 17, 2021: Black Farmers - If You Don't Know, Now You Know | The Daily Show - YouTube

The relief bill President Biden signed into law earlier in 2021 had $4 billion in loan forgiveness for black farmers. Which it turns out, a federal judge blocked.

With disgust in his voice, Fox News personality Tucker Carlson said, "Joe Biden sent millions of dollars to African American Farmers in this country, purely because of how they look. Now that's illegal. It's immoral. It's completely divisive."

Jon Stevens [owner of Maple Grove Farms] said on NEWSMAX, "It's not a bill for black farmers. It's a bill against white farmers."

In an interview on Fax News, Adam Faust stated, "I don't think they understand our business, one bit. Nobody asks you what race you are when you price fertilizer."

Another white lady said, "The democratic party is becoming the party of reverse racism."

On Fox News, on *Tucker Carlson Tonight*, Stephen Miller said: "Farmers are being denied aid, solely because of their skin color. In this country, you do not punish people. After all, they look a certain way because their ancestors come from a certain place. Because if the government has the power to destroy a business because of how someone looks,

What's next? Putting someone in jail for how they look?"

(This statement could be recited out of an African American farmer's mouth and be completely justified. But it came out of the mouth of a white man, and thus it is entirely tone-deaf.){pun intended} Black farmers and black people were and still are vastly discriminated against because of the color of their skin and because of the way they look, and because their ancestors came from a certain place. The government has sabotaged and destroyed many black- owned businesses because of how the owner's look. There has been and continues to be a large number of African Americans falsely imprisoned because of the way they look.)

In early June 2021, a federal judge blocked the aid from going into effect, while a lawsuit from white farmers proceeded through the court system.

Some people may still question: "Why should black farmers get special treatment"? There was a time in America when farming was very popular among black people. By force and by choice, black people have long and deep connections to American farmland. After the fall of slavery, owning a piece of land that could be worked and farmed symbolized freedom. During reconstruction, black folks saved their money. They worked together as families and as a cooperative. They bought the land that allowed black families to build communities, up to sixteen million acres.

At the peak of black farm ownership around 1920, maybe about 15% of farmers were African American. In a place where you could not vote, black folks could exert power by having some control over the land under their feet. Owning anything back then was incredible for black people. Don't forget that just one generation before that, black people were considered property, not even human. So, if there were so many black farmers back in the day, what happened to them? Answer: systemic racism.

White folks learned early on that one way to stop the Civil Rights Movement, one way to undercut it, was to get rid of land ownership. Over the last century, America's black farmers have lost more than 90% of their land because of systemic discrimination and a cycle of debt. The U.S. Department of Agriculture has a long history of discrimination. A study commissioned by the USDA found that loans to black male farmers were 25% lower than those given to white male farmers, on average.

For decades, the U.S. Department of Agriculture systematically favored white farmers by denying loans to black farmers. Discrimination was widespread at the USDA's local branches, which were run by all-white county committees. Many black farmers would come into the office, and the local official would say, "We don't have any money available." When white farmers came in, they would process their loans in less than thirty days, but for black farmers, it took 387 days on average. Black farmers would fill out the paperwork. Then the officials would take the paperwork and just throw it in the trash.

Without the same access to funds, black farmers struggled to keep up with their white competitors and were often forced out of business. We're talking $177 billion to $230 billion that black farmers have lost because of active discrimination.

That's right. For decades the USDA actively discriminated against black farmers, giving them smaller loans than white farmers or outright refusing to give them loans at all. That's how bad this discrimination was.

After decades of discrimination, black farmers had enough trauma and drama. They took their complaints right to the top. Black farmers first picketed the USDA in 1996. About fifty showed up with a pair of mules and a wagon to protest racial discrimination. Thousands had sent in complaints. They found the Office for civil rights, at the USDA had been closed for years, and boxes of their letters had remained unopened.

In 1999, thousands of black farmers settled a historic class-action discrimination lawsuit against the USDA in the landmark case "Pigford v Glickman." The government agreed to pay out more than $1 billion, with thousands of black farmers receiving upto $50,000 each. The vast majority never received a dime from the federal government.

An overwhelming number of farmers were dubbed as "Late Filers" by the USDA, when their applications trickled into the office in boxes after a 180-day deadline. Tens of thousands of black farmers claimed they did not receive proper notification after the settlement. For so many of them, it has been red tape and setbacks ever since. It has been eleven years of splitting time between the farm fields and Capitol Hill, staging protest, even riding tractors through downtown DC to get attention from Congress.

The government tried to fix things back in 2011 by providing funding to black farmers, but unfortunately, it came too late for many of them. It still fell far short of the economic losses that they had suffered at the hands of the USDA. So, the next time you hear people talking about how black farmers are getting "extra special" TREATMENT from the government, think about the TREATMENT they have been getting over the last 100 years. Some of the people who are upset about this loan forgiveness might not even know that all this discrimination even happened.

[MSNBC – *Justice for Black Farmers* (2021)]

The following is taken from:

Beyond Tulsa: The Secret History of Flooding Black Towns to Make Lakes | The Amber Ruffin Show – YouTube

"Over the past couple of years, more Americans have become familiar with the Tulsa Race Massacre, where a white mob burned a vibrant black community to the ground. Dozens of other black towns have been erased from the American map, not by burning them down but by hiding them underwater. Don't know what I mean?

Lake Lanier is in Forsyth County, Georgia, where people go swimming, boating, fishing, and other lake, waterfront activities. Before it was Lake Lanier, it was a town called Oscarville, Georgia. Then, Oscarville was a thieving, predominately black community, with a church, a school, and dozens of homes until the year 1912, when a very terrible thing happened. Two black teenagers were accused of rape. They were tried, convicted, and sentenced to death in a single day. After

72

they were executed, a mob of white men terrorized and drove out or killed all the black people in the surrounding area.

They did that until the entire black community of Oscarville disappeared. The county went from having over one thousand black residents in 1912, to zero in 1920. After all of the black people had been run off, the white people of Forsyth County said, you know what we could use? A big 'ole lake. So, they made one, right where the town had been. They flooded the area and literally covered the entire town with water. The town is still under the water. The homes, churches and schools are still down there under the water, and now people go boating on top of the town.

Kowaliga, AL was a black community. It is now Lake Martin.

York Hill, NY, was located in what is now Central Park Reservoir.

Seneca Village, NY, was located in what is now more of Central. Park

Henry and McKee Islands were located in what is now Lake Guntersville, AL

Vanport, OR, was located in

what is now Delta Park

Kennett, CA
Bird, CA

Elmore, CA

Morley, CA

Dearfield, CO: a Colorado ghost town that was once a bustling all-black settlement (nbcnews.com)

Sapinero, CO

Dillon, CO

Jerusalem, CO

Old Fairfield, IN

Round Valley, NJ

Warren, MD

Dana, MA

Enfield, MA

Greenwich, MA

Prentiss, MI

Brown's Station, NY

Old Neversink, NY

There are over one hundred drowned American towns. Many were destroyed in the name of something called development induced displacement. This is when people have to leave their homes so that the government can develop things like dams, parks, and lakes.

This happens to both black and white people. Historically, when it happens, black people and other people of color are under- compensated for their property or not compensated at all. The theory is that the short- term harmful effects are worth the long-term benefits for the community. But it is not fair if the long-term gain is mostly for white people.

If you are going to kick people out of their homes, make sure they have enough money to stay on their feet. The government should pay their descendants too, because generational wealth is one of the many things destroyed when you put black communities under water. These drowned towns are part of Black American history they don't teach you. It is ugly and gross, and we don't know all of it.

The more we find out, the harder it is to love this place that would do those things to so many people."

Please view:

Housing Discrimination: Last Week Tonight with John Oliver (HBO) - YouTube

Racism comes from EGO. Some people have the erroneous need to degrade others to make themselves feel better about themselves.

Jealously and envy are EGO emotions. They come from the compare & compete. Many white people will cut off their nose to spite their face and will do anything and everything to stop a black person from succeeding.

A quote from President Lyndon B. Johnson:

"If you can convince the lowest white man he's better than the best colored man, he won't notice you're picking his pocket. Hell, give him somebody to look down on, and he'll empty his pocket for you."

Now, what does that tell you about the ego of the white man?

The destruction of successful, thriving black communities was an extreme measure to prevent the truth from being proven and displayed; that black people are intelligent and civilized and capable of the same accomplishments as whites.

Currently, in corporate America, there is another glass ceiling for African Americans and even another for African American women. They have their hidden agenda ways of discouraging, preventing, and sabotaging African Americans in the workplace. Recently, many Fortune 500 corporation CEOs said they could not find any qualified African Americans to fill executive positions. Part of the cause for that problem is their hidden agenda mentioned previously; the micro aggressions, racial slurs, stealing of ideas, project sabotage, pranks, cruel jokes, and harassment.

Also, please read: ***1919, The Year of Racial Violence: How African Americans Fought Back*** by David F. Krugler.

As I stated earlier in this chapter, the conqueror gets to write or rewrite history to include or exclude anything he wants. But when the U.S. Attorney General said, "history is written by the winners," it took on a whole new meaning. We see a particular, specific group of people currently trying to re-write and spin the U.S. Capitol Insurrection of January 6, 2021, attempting to whitewash, vindicate, and pardon the events of that day. We see this same group of people causing controversy over teaching Critical Race Theory (CRT), misrepresenting its real definition. CRT is not taught in grade school or high school. CRT examines U.S. laws and how they have impacted different races. We see this same group of people distorting and misrepresenting Colin Kaepernick taking a knee during the national anthem at the beginning of football games.

Some white people want to think and teach their children to think that they are better than black people simply because of the color of their skin. They don't want to acknowledge the fact that slavery, Jim Crow, segregation, discrimination, intentional mental physical and spiritual sabotage, Red Lining Real Estate & Districting, lynching, beatings, murdering, destroyingthriving and affluent African American communities, the destruction of generational wealth, racial slurs, and micro- aggressions have caused African Americans to find themselves in economically inferior situations.

Dear white people and Mr. B. M.,

If becoming aware of the complete TRUE history of the United States makes you feel guilty or uncomfortable, then that's an issue to be discussed with your therapist. How you react to it and how it makes you feel, singularly, has to do with what is between your two ears.

Please don't confuse Critical Race Theory (CRT) with the complete TRUE history of the United States. The purpose of CRT is not to evoke feelings of guilt and discomfort.CRT is not taught in U.S. public schools K – 12. If you want to know what your kid is learning, go on your state's board of education website and look at the essential knowledge and skills that are required for each grade level.

The complete TRUE history of the United States has been distorted, parts deleted, and white-washed for centuries.

You shouldn't currently feel any guilt or discomfort about events that took place before you were born. But if **you are currently practicing** blatant racism, overt racism, blatant aggressions, micro-aggressions, terrorism, thievery, violence, discrimination, or sabotage against people or color, then your guilt and discomfort may be justified.

Definition:

Cognitive Dissonance: the perception of contradictory information. Cognitive dissonance is typically experienced as psychological stress when persons is presented with credible information that goes against their strongly held beliefs, which they considered to be unquestionable facts. According to this theory, when two actions or ideas are not psychologically consistent with each other, people do all in their power to change them until they become consistent.

White Fragility: discomfort and defensiveness on the part of a white person when confronted by information about racial inequality and injustice.

Many white people think they are morally and ethically

superior to people of color, and their economic advantages and privilege came from such superiority. Many white people don't want to acknowledge that the United States, from its inception, has blatantly implemented policies and laws that severely inhibit, and sabotage the efforts of black people. Of course, ego instigates and coaxes white people to want to feel superior to others.

Because the United States public school systems (K – 12) has intentionally done such a poor job of teaching the whole TRUTH about U.S. History, some white people are experiencing cognitive dissonance when confronted with the realization that they are not superior simply because of the color of their skin. They are not economically advantaged because they **think** they are more intelligent than people of color. Their forefathers created a full system of thorough indoctrination and institutionalized discrimination, which permeate the federal, state, local governments, and the private capitalist society.

Please view: The Racist Origins of U.S. Law - YouTube

Please read "*The Original Black Elites*" by Elizabeth DowlingTaylor

Please read "*White Fragility*" by Robin Diangelo

Sincerely, Eileena

There is a specific Friday night television host who thinks that slavery was "low key" an advantage for black people. He thinks that "in the big picture" and "in the long run," because Africans were shipped to the Americas from the 1600s to the 1800s, this has given twenty- first century African Americans much better life than if their ancestors had never left Africa.

People believe what they want to believe. They see what they want to see & notice (with ill intention and sarcasm) overemphasizing some of the primitive, indigenous spaces still on the African continent. Read these books: 1. *Stolen Legacy* by George J.M. James 2. *They Came Before Columbus* by Ivan Van Sertima 3. *The African Origin of Civilization: Myth or Reality* by Cheikh Anta Diop 4. *The Destruction of Black Civilization: Great Issues of a Race from 4500 B.C. to 2000 A.D* by: Chancellor Williams

When encountering the literature and information of complete, true history of the United States, how about conjuring up feelings of sympathy, empathy (if applicable), understanding, compassion, and passion to stand up and reverse the effects the white forefather's disgusting, despicable behavior, and discontinue your own blatant racism, overt racism, blatant aggressions, micro-aggressions, terrorism, thievery, violence, discrimination, or sabotage against people or color.

So, during Mr. B.M.'s comedy special, he brought up the fact that there were Africans who owned other Africans as slaves. He actually broached this subject matter in a comedy setting. Then when the audience began to cheer and clap, he discouraged them from doing so, and objected to their behavior.

Why would he even bring this up at a comedy show? What reaction did he expect? What reaction would have been appropriate (in general)? What reaction would have been appropriate in Mr. B.M.'s opinion?

In general, most Africans and African Americans know about blacks owning blacks as slaves, from the 1600s thru 1900s, in Africa and in the Americas. Most black people are quite familiar with black "sell outs" and "Uncle Toms." Most black people know that on the continent of Africa, some Africans helped capture other Africans, and sold them into slavery.

For some twisted and illogical reason, Mr. B. M. and other ignorant, misguided white people think these facts should somehow make African Americans feel less trauma, anger, disgust, anguish, and despair over the slave trade during the colonization of the Americas and the early beginnings of the United States.

As I have mentioned sever times, there are good people and bad people in every race.

Here is another intelligent and informed rebuttal to Mr. B.M's point of view on slavery, please view: Higher Learning YouTube channel: Discussing Slavery and Presentism, Plus Breaking Down the SAFE-T Act With Sen.Robert Peters - YouTube

: starting at 14:15 minutes to 47:36 minutes.

The desire to capture and enslave other human beings is

EGO NATURE not human nature.

There has always been slave abolitionist.

As a current citizen of the United States, I am only concerned with the history of the slave trade in the United States.

Speaking as an African American woman and as a descendant of black American farmers/landowners, and as a descendant of slaves, I fully blame the founding fathers of **THIS** country, writers of **THIS** country's laws, policies, and generally accepted practices and behaviors, Jim Crow laws, segregation, discrimination, terrorism, lynching, Red Lining real estate, blatant aggressions, micro aggressions, sabotage and thefts, which stripped away my families dignity, strength, wealth, education and legacy. Many African Americans share my same sentiments.

Because of the United States slave trade, most African Americans cannot even trace their ancestry back past the first generation outside of slavery.

The plight and condition of the majority of African Americans, currently, is a direct result of the United States slave trade.

So, if there was no United States slave trade, what would African American lives look like today, if Africans from the 1600s thru the 1900s, were asked if they would like to come to the Americas and be paid a fair wage for their labor, and be given humane or acceptable living quarters, home ownership opportunities, medical care and other benefits and citizenship, as a full human being? (as opposed to being considered 3/4th human)

One YouTuber has a video asking, Why aren't Black Lives Matter members protesting against Africans, Arabs, and Muslims as they all were former African slave owners and traders?

Answer: Black Lives Matter (started in the year 2013), it is a current social movement, to fight, (among many things), current police brutality and racially motivated violence.

Also, one group's enslavement and brutality against Africans does not absolve any other group's enslavement and brutality against Africans.

Please view: Jon Talks White Resentment w/ Isabel Wilkerson | The Problem With Jon Stewart Podcast | Apple TV+ - YouTube

Please view: "Let's talk about not seeing your black friends as black" – YouTube

Please view:
https://www.youtube.com/watch?v=E84OzHtEE8

OH KANYE: How The WEST Was Lost... - YouTube

To define the word woke, we must first understand the purpose of this endeavor and the context in which the word is being used. Is the word being used literally, figuratively, metaphorically, formally or as slang?

This is English and Communications 101.
The literal and formal definition of woke is past tense of wake (awake): an alert, aware and active state of consciousness.

Merriam-Webster defines sleep as the natural, easily reversible periodic state of many living things that is marked by the absence of wakefulness and by the loss of consciousness of one's surroundings, is accompanied by a typical body posture (such as lying down with the eyes closed), the occurrence of dreaming, and changes in brain activity and physiological functioning, is made up of cycles of non-REM sleep and REM sleep, and is usually considered essential to the restoration and recovery of vital bodily and mental functions.

Merriam-Webster defines awake as to arouse from sleep or a sleeplike state.

When a person is sleep, they often enter a dream state in which they believe they are conscious and experiencing reality. When they are awaken, they then realize what they thought was real, along with all the emotions, actions and reactions, was in fact not real at all. Some people cry when they awaken from nightmares. Some people feel relief when they wake up. Some people feel regret when they wake up. Some people feel a mixture of both relief and regret. Some people have a hard time facing reality after being awaken, because the dream seemed so vivid and so real, they had no doubt and were thoroughly convinced it was really happening. Their brain activity and physiological functions experienced the dream as real.

There are many stages, dimensions, and levels to sleep and consciousness. Just as there are many stages, dimensions, and levels to being awake, both figuratively and literally.

The slang woke and the slang conscious fit perfectly into this metaphor. The slang "being woke" means being awakened from what you thought was the truth and reality into a state of realization that you were mistaken about what is in fact true and what is in fact real.
As mentioned previously, there are many stages and levels to wokeness.

Being betrayed and becoming aware that someone you trusted is in fact untrustworthy is a level of wokeness. Being aware that hidden agendas are prevalent in every type of relationship (personal, professional, romantic) is a level of wokeness. Being aware of hidden agendas in religion, church leaders, government, politicians and secret societies is another level of wokeness.

Being liberal is not wokeness. Merriam-Webster defines liberal as: one who is open-minded or not strict in the observance of orthodox, traditional, or established forms or ways. Being accepting of the LGBTQIA+ community is not wokeness (In my opinion). It is a liberal point of view. A person can evolve and change their values, beliefs and point of view.

I can see how this could cause a disagreement of semantics. But I think many conservatives are being

intentionally asinine, disagreeable and trying to make the word woke a bad word with negative connotations.
Please keep in mind, as previously mentioned, there are many stages and levels to being woke.

****

People fear what they don't understand, and they hate what they fear. The cause and effect of this statement is: I resent the fact that I don't understand this thing, because it shows that I am lacking the required level of intelligence to understand this thing. I may also be at risk because of my lack of understanding. Because of my lack of understanding, I may not take the appropriate action to reduce or prevent my risk or venerability. I resent the fact that I don't understand this thing because apparently there are other people who do understand this thing and my intelligence must be "less than" in comparison to those who do understand.

CHAPTER THREE: AIN'T THAT THE NIGGER CALL'EN THE NIGGER A NIGGAH? IS HIP-HOP REALLY ART?

(Note: In this book, you will see many sentences, phrases, thoughts and messages repeated several times. This is intentional. Because we are so thoroughly indoctrinated, saturated and inundated with the follower's way of thinking and the "old" way of doing things; … new ideas, a new awareness, and the process of transitioning philosophies, thoughts, and lifestyle requires repetitive presentation.)

PROPERLY IDENTIFY THE PROBLEM

What do you think will happen to your subconscious if you keep pumping that angry, aggressive, negative message, negative vibration, negative frequency between your ears all day long? Did you know your subconscious is actually stronger than your conscious? What subliminal messages are being tattooed onto your subconscious mind and your brain cells?

There are many sub-genres within the genre of Hip-Hop/rap: Boom-Bap, Cloud Rap, Club, Conscious Rap, Crunk, Emo Rap, Gangster Rap, Jazz-Underground, Trap, Miami Trap, Midwest Chopper, Ol' School, and Reggaeton Rap, to name a few. You can't call it all bad, and you can't call it all good, either.

Which Hip-Hop sub-genres gets the most streaming, air-play and heavy rotation? … and WHY?

In the early days of hip hop, Ol' School and Conscious rap were the most popular, having positive and unifying messages.

If you really, really want to know the TRUTH and REALITY of what happened to the show-**business** part of the Hip-Hop, you can read:

The Psychological Covert War on Hip Hop by Professor Griff.

https://www.youtube.com/watch?v=26ORP uH1-rU

… if you really, really want to know… but most "followers" are blissfully and willfully living in ignorance. Most people are followers, and thus, they follow what is most popular. Most people are ego-driven, and they don't even realize and recognize that they can and should separate their ego from their true selves.

Great minds talk about ideas, mediocre minds talk about events, small minds talk about people.

What is the message in the most popular sub-genres of rap? Can we call it EGO RAP? It is mostly bragging about money and material possessions, insulting and degrading others, using and abusing women, using illegal drugs, and violence.

This has been called "Art" (?), a creative form of expression.

Yes, Hip-Hop is art, and every art form has an appropriate time and place. Some art forms have no place in my life. I choose not to consume art that puts me on a negative vibration. The year when I intentionally was celibate, I chose not to listen to slow jams and love songs because I knew the mood and vibe it would create. This is also why I don't listen to very much hip-hop other than Ol' School and conscious rap. I know the mood and vibe it will create.

Great minds talk about ideas. Mediocre minds talk about events. Small minds talk about people. (gossip)

In the early 1990s, Ms. C. Delores Tucker, a civil rights activist, very publicly spoke out against "Gangster Rap." The hip-hop audience was split, especially since the very popular and articulate Tupac Shakur had a well-publicized debate with Ms. C.D. Tucker on the issue. The crux of this debate was whether this is art and does the essence of the First Amendment, freedom of speech, apply? The answer to both questions is yes, but there is an appropriate time and place to display this art. This art is unsuitable for some people with regard to age, maturity, and with regard to other mental states and wellness.

I remember back in the early 1990s, my husband (at that time) brought home a CD of an artist who was using profanity and dissing women. My husband got such a big kick out of blasting this music so loud and cussing in my face, like an angry little boy with a shiny new toy. The males seem to like the shock value and they like to offend others by blasting this music—the EGO of it all. The other day, my niece and I were talking about the recently aired BET Awards. I said that most of the performances were nasty, raunchy, dirty, and sexually explicit. She asked me why I use those words to describe the dancers and choreography presented. She said it is just our "culture." She said the dances came from Africa and that African dancers move the same way. I disagreed with her. I said the dancers on the BET Awards (as with the majority of dancers) and the dancers in the sexually explicit videos are interpreting and/or enhancing the **lyrics** and music they are accompanying. If the lyrics are nasty, raunchy, dirty, and sexually explicit, then the accompanying dance is likely to be nasty, raunchy, dirty, and sexually explicit.

So, if you look at the Hip-Hop dancers and performances ON MUTE (with no sound), are you thinking, "Wow! This is beautiful, heritage-rich African Art?" Probably not.

Every art form has an appropriate time and place. The most popular forms of hip-hop are not for children's consumption. Most of the hip-hop performances presented on the BET Awards and most music award shows should not be viewed or heard by children. In my opinion, that kind of art belongs in a burlesque show or in a strip club. Adult entertainment belongs in adult settings.

The Grammy's have an award for the spoken word. These awards are given for poetry, audiobooks, and storytelling. Why can't African American award shows have award categories for conscious rap and other forms of the spoken word? I remember when rap mainly was about dancing, partying and having fun without degrading or insulting others. The current popular artists seem to want to see how low they can go to maximize shock value.

There is a gay YouTuber who has been releasing his own hip hop music. I must admit I haven't heard his entire catalog, but the cuts I have heard are braggadocios and degrading to others. Maybe he has songs about how invigorating and emancipating it is to be out of the closet or telling gay youths it gets better or telling them to always, consistently and vigorously support each other. Does he even realize there are other sub- genres to rap music or is he in it just to maximize his income.

The lyrics are practically the same within the most popular hip-hop sub-genres on streaming services and in the heaviest rotation. The videos are almost the same, degrading others, bragging about you and who you're screwin'. Some hip-hop want's to take LOVE out of romantic relationships. You know the lyrics, "… he doesn't love'em tho." They made it as though a man was a punk or weak to love, care for, and truly respect a woman. Some people called this the intentional destruction of the black family.

Were all the rhymes on the game show "Drop the Mike" insults? Degrading? And disses?

Within Hip-Hop culture, what was the point of that MTV show "*Yo Mamma*" or the show "*Comedy Knock Out*"? Just Jokes? There is a big difference between laughing at someone and laughing with someone. They are playing very close to the line and often crossing the line into being mean spirited. It is very childish, juvenile and ego-driven.

I love stand-up comedy and often go to live shows. I pick who I patronize carefully. Often unskilled comedians just go into angry rants, degrading and insulting others. This is not comedy. There are videos online from a comedy club in L.A. where this one particular female comedian's whole set was degrading and belittling men. They try to intertwine insults with humor, so they can say, "It's just jokes." But it is just a cheap way to capture audience members who may have the same simpleton gripes as the comedian. As I said, there is a big difference between laughing at someone and laughing with someone. You should recognize the ego-driven person who has the sick need to degrade others to make themself feel better about themselves.

Self-esteem and self-worth should not be based on material possessions and monetary accumulations. Self-esteem and self-worth should be based on doing the best you can with what you've been given. People who brag and show off are the kind of people who base their self-worth all or in part on other people's opinions. They are trying to impress and gain the approval of others, or on the other hand, they are trying to make others jealous.

Many genres of art are born out of heartache, anger, and frustration. Many rap artists express anger and frustration stemming from growing up in poverty or abusive situations. Unfortunately, children are taught, or they observe and then erroneously believe that self-worth and self-esteem should be based on material possessions. Another adverse effect of the materialistic measure of self-worth is that when people live in poverty, they think of themselves as worthless. They do the compare and compete. And when they compare themselves to someone who has more, it generates feelings of shame and worthlessness. This is why the compare and compete should not be done. This is why self-worth and self-esteem should not be based on material possessions.

Every form of art has an appropriate time and place. On the streaming services, radio, and any place with open unrestricted access, it is not suitable for most hip-hop. Parents should use parental control for radio, streaming services, the internet and television. Then let the market correct itself {supply & demand}. Without exposure and heavy streaming and heavy rotation, the demand will be lowered. Then maybe those aspiring rap artists will realize they need an education, marketable skills and a "Plan B" as an alternate means to earn a living.

There are thousands of success stories of people who have made it out of poverty through legal means with education and hard work. The key is to believe that YOU CAN DO IT! Don't let unfortunate circumstances and obstacles hold you back. Maybe, you had no control over the family into which you were born. Your self-esteem and self-worth should be based on TRULY doing the best you can with what you've been given. Your higher power birthed you into your family and surrounding circumstances for specific reasons and for you to learn specific life lessons because you have a stronger soul and can handle the struggle and fight to get out.

You have a billion-dollar brain. Remember, most people only use 10% of their brain capability during their lifetime. You should USE MORE!

In the United States, it is the LAW for children to go to school until they are between sixteen and eighteen years of age (it varies by state). IT IS THE LAW! The government sends officers after children and parents to ensure that the child goes to school. They are called Truant Officers. In other countries, especially in many Third World countries, children don't even complete grade school. They have to work to support their families. Often children are sold into prostitution or other forms of slavery.

Oprah Winfrey did a special show on a trip she took to Africa. She visited these two sisters (orphans), who could not go to school. One reason they could not go to school was that they did not have school uniforms. These children had no adults in their home. They were struggling to keep their shack for shelter and working for food and water. Oprah asked the eldest girl what she wanted most. Of all the things the girl could have said food, water, shelter), she said school uniforms because without uniforms, the girls were not allowed to go to school.

Oprah built a school for girls in South Africa. She was asked why she didn't create a school in the United States. She replied: (paraphrasing) because it is the law for children to go toschool in the U.S.

As much as we complain about our education system and as much as our education system is indeed flawed, we have it so much better than many other places on this planet. We need to take full advantage of what we have. We need to do the best we can with what we have been given.

Self-esteem should not be based on being the most popular, being a follower, being in the hip or popular clique, or on other people's opinions. If the parents can grasp this concept, believe it, and live by it, the children will learn it, believe it, and live by it.

Unfortunately, elementary school children get so caught up in materialism, and the compare and compete leads to self-esteem issues at such a young age. They learn it from their parents. Some children living in poverty develop low self-esteem and get distracted from their schoolwork and then poor grades further compound the problem.

Many rappers rap about the struggles of living in

crime and poverty stricken circumstances. There is real mental anguish that comes from living in these circumstances. Many songs in many different genres of music are written about losing someone you love, and the hurt and mental anguish experienced. This is all creative expression in the form of art. Remember, there is a higher power. Never be so arrogant to believe you can control all circumstances surrounding you. There are many popular sayings such as, "The Lord giveth andthe Lord taketh away", and

"God helps those who help themselves," and "Easy come, easy go."

Everyone (rappers included) should remember that wealth can be given or allowed by your higher power and can be taken away by your higher power. Don't take your wealth for granted. Always have a backup plan. Can you cope with losing your wealth? Do you have a backup plan, another set of marketable skills, an education? If your self-esteem is based (even in part) on material possessions or monetary wealth …and you lose that wealth, will you be devastated?

In every sector of business and place of employment, people compare and compete. In rap music, there is an abundance of degrading and belittling one another, words of anger, threats, acts of violence, and murder.

If your self-worth and self-esteem are based on the right thing, you won't feel the need to degrade and belittle another person to pump yourself up.

Whether spoken or unspoken, conscious or sub-conscious, a person knows if they have real substance and real talent. A defense mechanism for a person who does not have real substance and real talent is to degrade and belittle someone else to throw the attention off themselves and onto someone else. Then they won't be scrutinized and evaluated, and THE TRUTH of their minuscule substance and minuscule talent won't be revealed.

Parents should sensor and control the material to which their children are exposed. But some exposure will happen beyond the parent's control. Parents can explain to their children that it is unfortunate, yet it is very real that people are born and live in crime-ridden, dirty, scary, abusive environments. They should also explain that some people never learn or figure out that there are legal, positive and productive ways to deal with their situation and get out of it. Unfortunately, they never learned the right way to deal because along the way, someone did tell them they could be whatever they wanted to be. They were advised to stay focused and work hard to reach their goals. They succumbed to peer pressure, followed the crowd, and let others hold them back.

Parents should explain to their children that it is unfortunate that some people think it is necessary to brag, boast, and flaunt their material possessions because they never understood their self-worth and self-esteem should not be based on material possessions. If you obtain these things illegally or unethically, they will eventually be taken from you. If you base your self-esteem on these things and they are taken from you, you will be emotionally devastated, and it will be hard to recover.

What is the average career span of a rapper?

Do you know how to calculate an average?

Do you know how to calculate a probability?

Parents should further explain to their children that rappers have every right to express themselves through the art of rapping. Then further explain that there is a bigger picture surrounding this art

… **REAL LIFE!**

Explain to your sons that they should not abuse and degrade females just because they hear someone do it BOLDLY in a song. It doesn't translate well into **REAL LIFE**. Parents explain to your daughters that if they base their self-esteem on the right thing, they won't need to sell their soul, sell their self-respect, perform degrading and demeaning acts to get a man's attention and affection.

People who are mature, secure, and self- assured don't need to degrade, belittle, use and abuse others to make themselves feel better or for any other reason. People of real substance and real talent do not need to brag, boast, show off, or draw attention to themselves. It will be obvious to other people who have real substance and real talent. Game recognizes game.

If your art is to bring a script for a play or a movie to life, you might be satisfied working with your local theatre company or creating your own independent movies. Check the true motivation. Does your ego feed off of cheering crowds, many admiring eyes on you, people clambering and chaos trying to get to you? Do you want the biggest house in Beverly Hills?

My mother and I were at the salon getting pedicures when a young man came in asking us to go to his social media page to listen to his music. He played some of his music from his phone. He sounded pretty good. I asked him to sing "Ribbon in the Sky" by Stevie Wonder. He was unfamiliar with the song.

(I don't care how young or old you are, "Ribbon in the Sky" is R&B 101. You godd'ah know "Ribbon in the Sky") Stevie's version is exquisite. The group Intro's version is fire.

I asked him if he knew about the dark side of the music industry. He said yes, he had heard that some people sell their souls for a recording contract. I asked him if he could read and write music. He said no. He said he just records his original work on his phone. I asked him if he was hoping to get famous and make a lot of money or just enjoy sharing his art of music with people. He said both. I suggested he go back to school, earn a degree in performing arts, learn to read and write music, learn to play an instrument, and plan what he is going to do when they put that fat contract in front of his face and ask him: "What do you really want?" How much money is enough?

Are you comparing and competing to have the biggest and baddest material possessions and to make others jealous?

Properly identify the problem.

Check your true motives. Streaming services, radio stations, music video stations and DJs do have a choice. But the "followers" follow the crowd and follow the money.

A popular hip-hop artist wants to change the law regarding the penalty for possession and distribution of certain forms of cocaine. The effort is to equalize the penalty for possession of powder cocaine and crack cocaine. Because the penalty is stiffer for crack cocaine, minorities are unfairly experiencing tougher sentencing than others convicted of possession and distribution of powder cocaine.

I don't know if I agree with changing this law because if an individual chooses to break the law, they already know there are consequences for breaking the law. It doesn't matter if someone else should have, could have, would have received a lighter sentence for a similar crime.

IF YOU CHOOSE TO BREAK THE LAW, THERE ARE CONSEQUENCES!

With all his power, popularity, and influence, I feel this hip hop artist could put his energy and efforts to better use by helping to educate and retrain these drug dealers so they can get legal, productive, self-fulfilling careers.

PROPERLY IDENTIFY THE PROBLEM

Is the real problem unequal sentencing? Or is the real problem these drug dealers have their egos and self-esteem based on money and material possessions or fitting in with a particular crowd and being popular. They followed the crowd in school, wasted their time, didn't learn what they needed to learn, didn't gain the marketable skills they should have gained, and saw selling drugs as a quick fix and a way to get big money.

There is too much risk involved with being a drug dealer. The risk of losing your freedom, the risk of having a felony/criminal record follows you for the rest of your life, the risk of the psychological and physical effects of incarceration, the risk of putting your life and your family's lives in danger, the moral di- lemma/ irresponsibility of enabling drug addiction; causing sickness and death, destroying lives and destroying families and communities.

Some people offer the excuse of, "I needed to put food on the table." There are many legal ways to provide for the bare necessities. But most drug dealers are driven by EGO and are going for bragging rights, fancy clothes, large bling, lux automobile, control, and power.

Some people say, "I did the best I could" or "I tried my best." They use these lines as an excuse for failure. Ask yourself HONESTLY, did you put adequate time, effort, research, analysis and proper work into whatever you

85

were trying to accomplish?

Be honest with yourself. You have to be truly honest about doing your very best, because in your private moments when you face yourself when you face the truth and reality, if you have to admit to yourself, "Damn, I really could have done more" or "I really could have put more time and effort into that" or "I know I held back for some selfish reason" then your self-esteem will be lowered. And you may not know the right way to pick yourself back up.

Your self-esteem should be based on doing the best you can with what you've been given. This is only a good and positive thing if you can be honest with yourself and live an honest life-style.

Nobody is perfect. We all make mistakes. You will be more willing and able to forgive yourself if you can be honest and know that the mistake was not intentional and not devious.

CHAPTER FOUR: GET OVER IT, DARKY! SHADES OF DARKNESS

Black on Blacker Discrimination

(Note: In this book, you will see many sentences, phrases, thoughts and messages repeated several times. This is intentional. Because we are so thoroughly indoctrinated, saturated and inundated with the follower's way of thinking and the "old" way of doing things; … new ideas, a new awareness, and the process of transitioning philosophies, thoughts, and lifestyle requires repetitive presentation.)

The first step in problem-solving is to PROPERLY IDENTIFY THE PROBLEM.

1. Is the problem that more employment opportunities/promotions are given to lighter African Americans than darker African Americans?

2. Is the problem that a man/woman prefers a lighter African American than a darker African American man/woman for romantic and sexual relationships?

3. Is the problem that parents and grandparents show favorable/preferential treatment to the lighter child over the darker child?

The answer to all three is: no

… Well …yes, these are problematic circumstances and symptoms of the real true problem. If you think these three questions are indicative of real issues, my next question for you would be: issues for whom?

Your self-esteem should be based on: Doing _____with given.

(You've got this by now. Right?)

Your self-esteem should not be based on other people's opinions.

Most of us (no matter our color) have had job opportunities or advancement opportunities slip away from us. Most of us (no matter our color) have liked, desired, or loved someone who did not reciprocate the feelings. These things happen often across the globe. We generally accept them as a part of the full spectrum of life.

In a later chapter in this book, I get into a deep discussion on female self-image issues. (spoiler alert) I point out how the skinny models in the magazines are not the problem. The properly identified problem is the basis of the magazine reader's self-esteem. Is the reader comparing and competing with the model in the magazine?

Not to throw shade, (I very much appreciate the intent and the effort) but there were several programs on a particular minority female's network regarding colorism amongst brown and black people and also racism in general. It seemed that people on each extreme of melanation and all hues in between were all commiserating about the challenges each sector experienced. I guess the intent was to gain sympathy and empathy from the "others" in the room. Each group felt the "others" had advantages associated with their shade of color, and each group wanted the "others" to understand the issues faced by their particular group. I really didn't see any solid solutions offered.

The solution is to base your self-esteem on the right thing. Don't do the compare and compete. The solution is to learn to recognize your EGO and understand that EGO and self- esteem have two very different definitions.

You can fly and soar far above the problems indicated in the first three questions of this chapter by mastering the law of attraction to attract the career of your choice and attracting the mate or partner of your choice.

But even before all of that, you might want to narrow down: what the purpose of this lifetime is for you? What life lessons am I supposed to learn during this incarnation of my soul? What am I supposed to accomplish with this soul's embodiment?

You are a divine spiritual being having a temporary human experience. Look in the mirror and say: "This is the vessel with which my creator blessed me to journey through this lifetime. My creator knows what is best for me and has equipped me with everything I need to successfully navigate through this lifetime. I have no regrets or qualms about this vessel because I am not comparing or competing with any other vessels. My vessel [ca] is uniquely mine, just as my missions and assignments for this lifetime are uniquely mine, therefore, to compare and compete is pointless."

Perhaps you are not meant to be coupled or procreate during this lifetime. The followers have their list of accomplishments, achievements, and experiences that they say we should all "check off" the list as we pass through our twenties, thirties, forties, and so on. But those items may not be meant for you, for your specific journey through this specific lifetime. You don't have to follow the crowd.

… And now I will appeal to your ego …

Many people find darker skin more appealing. Some are willing to express and act on these feelings, and some are too weak and embarrassed to do so. We should strive to live above that shallow, superficial behavior in the most literal way.

There is a reason "they" want to be like us, imitate us, look like us, speak like us, dance like us, and appropriate our culture. They say imitation is the highest form of flattery. Envy is part of their hatred toward us. The excessive hair flipping makes me laugh. When I see it, I think to myself, I can gauge the magnitude of this hair flipper's ego and adjust my interaction strategy. Appealing to their ego may be useful in my hidden agenda.

(Funny story … I was upset and filing a complaint with customer service. The CS representative thought she could calm me down or charm me out of my complaint by flooding me with compliments. Well, yes, she did make me laugh (de-fused and de-escalated). I laughed because I saw straight through her strategy, and I said to myself, "Ok Bitch, I see what you're try'en to do here, and I'm not swayed or distracted by your fake-ass flattery. Now back to processing my refund."]

… But I digress …

… now, back to the three questions from the beginning of this chapter …

The first step in problem-solving is to PROPERLY IDENTIFY THE PROBLEM.

QUESTION #1: Is the problem that more employment opportunities/promotions are given to lighter African Americans than darker African Americans?

Here are some HARSH, WELL-ESTABLISHED FACTS:

Statistically, Caucasians get paid higher salaries than African Americans for the same jobs with equivalent credentials.

Statistically, men get paid higher salaries than women for the same jobs with equivalent credentials.

Statistically, obese applicants get selected less often than healthy weight applicants. Statistically, attractive applicants get chosen more often than less attractive applicants, and attractiveness is subject to individual taste.

Statistically, more employment opportunities/promotions are given lighter African Americans than darker African Americans.

Yes, these are statistical facts, and yes, these could be real problems if you allow them to be.

Don't wallow in anger and frustration. Negative energy attracts negative situations and circumstances.

Insert the serenity prayer, "Lord, help me change the things I can change, accept the things I cannot change, and grant me the wisdom to know the difference."

Can you change any of these statistics?

You might be able to make a small change, if you are confronted with this type of discrimination individually and want to pursue legal action (if allowed). You can make monetary contributions or volunteer your time at organizations that fight these types of discrimination.

So, can you sue because more employment

opportunities/promotions are given lighter African Americans than darker African Americans? Probably not. You can talk about it till you're blue in the face, but you probably cannot change it. You can raise awareness, but you have minimal control or influence over an employer's preferences, opinions, and actions in this situation. Your energies would be better spent developing and mastering marketable skills and making yourself as well-groomed and prepared for interviews as possible.

Don't go into an interview with negative energy, a bad attitude, and a chip on your shoulder.

The real world is not perfect. Some situations are unfair and uncomfortable. It would be best if you dealt with these situations in the most mature and professional manner possible. Use positivity and the law of attraction to attract the career you want. Don't dwell on negativity. Let it go.

Sometimes darker women complain that they are insulted when they receive a complement from someone saying: "You are gorgeous for a dark person."

I have received this compliment in the

past; I am a darker African American woman. And my response is to graciously smile and say thank you, as my mother taught me to use good manners and not read any more or any less into the situation.

Why do some women react the same to the compliment "You are gorgeous for a dark person" as you would react to someone insulting you by calling you darkie or blacky? One statement comes from a sincere person with no ill intentions. It just may not be the best choice of words, and they are sending a positive message. The other statement comes from a negative person intending to put you down and bring you down. An adverse reaction is an ego reaction.

Your self-image, self-esteem, self-worth should 100% NOT be based on another person's opinion.

QUESTION # 2:

Is the problem that a man/woman prefers Lighter African American man/woman more often than Darker African American man/woman?

PROPERLY IDENTIFY THE PROBLEM ...

Is this REALLY a
problem?

If so, whose problem is it?

Every individual has the right to their own personal preference. And your preference doesn't need to be explained or justified to any other person.

Why is it ok for some people to prefer spicy food over lightly seasoned food? Why is it ok for a person to prefer contemporary jazz as opposed to renaissance jazz? Is it ok for a person to prefer the feel of silk over cashmere? With your five senses, you are certainly allowed to have your preferences of what you like to taste, what kind of music you want to listen to, what you like to feel against your skin, and so forth...

Some people will have a preference for you, and some will not. And that works both ways. Are you attracted to every person you encounter?

I overheard a conversation between two young ladies speaking about a class reunion. One young lady was distraught because a tight group of friends (African American men) each one had married "light-skinned, petite" females. I thought to myself, it is none of her business who these men chose for their wives.

Yes, she does have a right to her own opinion. But what is her opinion based on? And why expend negative energy and negative emotion and draw negative energy to herself over an issue that is absolutely none of her business?

My guess is that these brotha's compared and competed with their girlfriends, fiancés and wives. My guess is EGO played a big part in these choices. And they will have to deal with the consequences of these choices, whether good or bad.

Marrying someone ONLY because of physical attraction is (in my opinion) a bit shallow, and the relationship may not last because it has no depth. But physical attraction is rarely the ONLY reason for marriage.

If women/men of a lighter complexion appeal to you, this does not have to be explained or justified to anyone else.

And likewise, if women/men of a darker complexion appeal to you, this does not have to be explained or justified to anyone else. Don't let your ignorant, immature friends and/or family shame you out of a relationship with your soulmate.

Guess what! There ARE people with darker skin complexions who are, IN FACT, intelligent, compassionate, philosophical, analytical, beautiful - in every sense of the word, and they deserve to be loved and adored as much as anyone else!!!!!

…and Guess What!

There ARE people with lighter skin complexions who are, IN FACT, intelligent, compassionate, philosophical, analytical, and beautiful - in every sense of the word. They also deserve to be loved and adored as much as anyone else!

People often say that the media and fashion magazines influence the popular definition of "BEAUTY." This may or may not be true.

PROPERLY IDENTIFY THE PROBLEM. The media is not the problem. The problem lies within each individual and the basis of their self-esteem. Are you being a follower? Are you comparing and competing?

If a person develops an eating disorder trying to look more like a model in a fashion magazine {being a follower}, the basis of her self-esteem and self-worth is

THE PROBLEM. The magazine is not the problem.

Not every person you meet will find you physically attractive. Some people will find your particular skin complexion more appealing than others. Your self-esteem should not be based on other peoples' opinions. Don't be mad if {for whatever reason(maybe skin color)} someone doesn't find you attractive.

If you lose your partner to someone with a lighter skin complexion because of the skin complexion, then you are better off without that former partner. It is more likely that there were much deeper problems within your relationship.

If you are jealous and resentful toward people with a lighter complexion than you, THE PROPERLY IDENTIFIED PROBLEM lies with you and the basis of your self-esteem and self-worth. Don't do the compare and compete to determine or gauge your self-esteem and self-worth. They had no control over the skin color with which they were born, just as you had no control over the skin color your creator gave you.

If physical attraction tops the list of many items that are important to an individual in choosing a mate, this individual's personal preference does not have to be explained or justified to anyone.

If the physical attraction keeps the

passion alive and keeps you faithful, then it's a good thing. Physical attraction is more important to some people and less necessary to others. It doesn't necessarily mean that one group is more mature or more philosophically astute than the other.

COMPATIBILITY in morals, religion/spirituality, philosophies, short and long-term career & personal goals, maturity level, sexuality are among a list of important items that sustain a lasting relationship.

QUESTION #3: Do parents and grandparents show favoritism toward lighter children over darker children?

How a child is treated by their parents/guardians has the greatest influence on how the child will treat others. Parents should put an extraordinary amount of effort to treat all children equally. If you see others treating your child adversely, you must correct them.

Teach your children that the content of their character is the true measure of their substance and self-worth, not the color of their skin. And the content of their character can make them beautiful on the inside as well as the outside. Teach them not to compare and compete" to determine their self-esteem. Teach them that their life's purpose is to use their brain to the fullest capability, to find and use the special and unique gifts God has given them to enhance and change the world.

Teach them that they are not their ego when they are intellectually able to comprehend this concept. Teach them that their self-esteem and self-worth should be based on doing the best they can with what they've been given.

PART 2:

RUNNING FOR OFFICE POLITICS

CHAPTER FIVE: COLLEGE IS FOR EVERY- ONE!!! WE CAN ALL HAVE A PIECE OF THE PIE!

(Note: In this book, you will see many sentences, phrases, thoughts and messages repeated several times. This is intentional. Because we are so thoroughly indoctrinated, saturated and inundated with the follower's way of thinking and the "old" way of doing things; ... new ideas, a new awareness, and the process of transitioning philosophies, thoughts, and lifestyle requires repetitive presentation.)

As an employer looking at résumés, I can see that this person has successfully set a ** LONG-TERM** goal (of three to six years) and has overcome obstacles, distractions, and setbacks to successfully reach this goal.

As a businesswoman and employer, I want a partner and employees who plan to stay with me and work with me for the **LONG - TERM**.

Can you focus for the long-term? Or are you all over the place in the long term? How stable are you?

Some scientists believe most humans only use about 10% of their brain capability during their lifetime. If an individual wants to be an Independent, self-supporting adult, with the high cost of living these days, that individual needs the kind of education and employment that will enable an independent and self- supporting lifestyle.

Think about this ... Most people spend their life (from age twenty to age sixty-five) in the workforce. Most people spend an average of forty-five years working before retirement.

*Seriously! * Just think about this. Forty-Five years working. Of those forty-five years, you CAN devote a measly five to eight years to education. And think about this: Where do you want to spend those forty-five years? At a minimum-wage job? Forty-five years in a minimum wage job? Do you want to spend forty- five years working your butt off, barely making ends meet? Forty-five years working two or three jobs at a time, still barely breaking even? Or burning out with no free time? Where is the quality of life?

I still have ten to fifteen years that I must work until retirement. I am still earning certificates and degrees. I need to get a promotion. Do you know why? Because my 401K, retirement savings and investment portfolio have suffered severely in this economy. I need to make more money. For these next fifteen years working until retirement, I need to rake in loads of money to rebuild my retirement funds.

Bill Gates did go to college. He didn't complete it, but he went. If a person has the opportunity to make "Bill Gates" kind of money, LEGALLY, by all means, DO IT!

Here is where people start to get left behind: in elementary school. If a child senses they are not learning at the same rate as other children, they will fake it. The child develops defense mechanisms to cover their shortcomings. Parents and teachers need to take a more active role in helping each child and challenging each child. Children have to learn how to learn. They have to learn how to sit still and focus. Parents should check their children's homework and hold the teachers to a higher standard. Community after-school programs, mentoring and tutoring programs are the solutions.

Some people say they are bad at taking tests. The solution to that is to take self-enrichment classes on "Taking Tests." Go on the internet and find practice tests and drills. Figure out your best learning style, for example: visually, audibly, tactile - by touch (hands-on).

While in graduate school, a friend laughed at me after finding a small portable cassette recorder/player in my car. I explained that I used the cassette recorder as a studying tool. I would tape myself reading the required text, then read the text again as I listened to the tape. He laughed again and said, "That sounds like a whole lot of work."

Of course, my feelings were NOT hurt because my self-esteem is not based (not even in part) on his opinion. Though unusual, this method of recording myself reading worked for me.

Some people can read, comprehend, and retain what they have read in the first go around. I can't, especially when reading several chapters at a time. I figured out what worked for me with the equipment I had, and I used it, and it worked, and still works.

One of the reasons most people are followers is because "LEARNING" is "AN ACT OF FOLLOWING." But after you reach a certain age (~eleven years old), you should recognize your individuality. Parents should encourage children to discover their own individuality. Parents have to teach their children to base their self-worth on the right things.

We have seen or experienced when a child reaches a certain age and starts to question everything. They want to know Why? ... and to that answer, they ask Why? ... and to that answer, they ask Why? Again... and to that answer, they ask Why? They also start early, trying to fit in and blend in with the crowd. Of course, they should be friendly and have friends, but they should also learn to think independently. They should be taught not to be afraid to stand alone, to be strong, and take a stand when they know they are right.

College is for everyone. Each person should have more than one set of UNRELATED marketable skills. This will make you more versatile and agile in the job market and will give you more options. Everyone should know business law and accounting. It is inevitable you will experience the need for this knowledge, when opening or operating a business, with your personal finances and any contract you sign.

Can we equate and draw a parallel between your highest level of mathematical education and your real-life problem-solving skills? When solving personal or professional relationship issues, are you capable when there are additional digits, variables, radicals, exponents, functions, axes, and dimensions? How are your problem-solving skills when you add more people, issues, emotional ties, loyalties, ethics, logic and fairness?

People often say they don't want to waste time learning subjects they may never use. My response to that is, the economy is global now, in the twenty-first century. You will likely attend professional functions with various people in a variety of locations, domestic and foreign. You should be able to speak intelligently and confidently about many different topics. This will serve you well when networking, mingling, and socializing.

As I said before: concerning spending the time in college; most people spend their life from the age of twenty to the age of sixty- five in the work force. Most people will spend an average of forty-five years working before retirement. Think about this: forty-five years. Of those forty-five years, you can devote a measly five to eight years to education. And where do you want to spend those forty-five years? Barely making ends meet?

Attending college for four, five, or more years, and earning at least one degree, should also help you attain other practical character attributes, such as patience. You will also learn howto stay focused on a long-term goal, overcome obstacles, and learn problem- solving and decision-making skills. Some people get so caught up in the compare and compete wanting to "keep up with the

Jones's." They want to instantly have house, fancy car and fine clothes. And they get jealous of those people who have these things, especially those who obtain these things at a very young age. But they (themselves) have not acquired marketable skills to facilitate earning money to purchase these items. Be patient. They are driven by jealously and ego. (Men are competing: I have to have the fancy clothes and the car to get the girl.)

And most importantly, you will get something from formal will not get from a trade school or on-the- job training, that is: effective communication skills.

1.ADVANCED VOCABULARY - Can you grasp education, college specifically, that you the message and understand when someone speaks to you with an advanced vocabulary?

2.SPEAKING PROPERLY - Do you use proper grammar when you speak? Can you put your thoughts into logical, grammatically correct, complete sentences?

(I have seen some educated African Americans "dumb down" their speaking capabilities to "fit in" with under-educated African Americans, "Speaking Black" because some ignorant person said they were "Speaking White." This is a form of the Crabs in a Barrel" mentality. The ignorant people are {in essence} saying: Stay ignorant like me. Speak poorly like me, so I won't feel so bad about being dumb and ignorant and incapable of speaking properly. I want to feel like I'm among a group of ignorant people because misery loves company. Followers love company.)

3.READING and COMPREHENSION - Can you read and understand literature written with an advanced vocabulary? Can you read and follow instructions? Can you read and understand a legally binding contract? Do you understand? Grasp the concept?

4.WRITING – Can you write logical, grammatically correct, complete sentences and a logically, well-structured paragraph? Can you write a business report, a business plan, a business proposal, an article, a research paper? Can you write your version of an incident or event?

Writing can also be very therapeutic. You can express your thoughts and feelings, sort things out and see if you can understand why you feel the way you do.

if you did not acquire all these skills from your college experience, you got cheated, or you cheated yourself. If you don't have all of these skills, you need to get them, fast. Register for classes or buy *Hooked on Phonics*. I'M NOT JOKING!

As a part of an interview process for a particular job, I was required to write a report. I was given random information relating to a topic and instructed to write a three-page report. I started by creating an outline listing key points in chronological order. I wrote an introductory paragraph, briefly mentioning each key point. Then I wrote two paragraphs for each key point. And finally, I wrote a summary paragraph, which looked very similar to the introductory paragraph, but with a few more details and a conclusion/recommendation.

This was for an accounting job, jot a journalism or communications job. I was not tested on preparing financial statements, principles of accounting, or mathematical skills. Every person in every profession should be able to do this. Writing is fundamental.

BTW …

… I got the job.

COLLEGE IS FOR EVERYBODY

Financing college may be challenging, but it is not impossible. Starting at a community college is nothing for which to be ashamed. Start with the financial aid office at your school of choice. Go online. Go to religious, Greek, and social organizations for educational, financial assistance. Find an employer who offers tuition assistance or reimbursement. Most colleges and universities have payment plans where you can make payments during each semester and pay off each semester as you go.

Remember, most people only use 10% of their brain's capability in their lifetime. Let's shoot for a passing grade of 80% or higher.

I have seen athletes, singers and rappers in interviews who have trouble putting their thoughts into meaningful sentences to answer questions. They should be able to read and understand their contracts - They – themselves – in addition to their lawyers and accountants.

That's why your self-esteem should not be based on money and material possessions or your job title. It's about substance. For whatever reason (even at the will of your higher power), you might lose your money, material possessions, or your job. Do you have a Plan B? Do you have other marketable skills? You may get fired, arrested, incarcerated, or go bankrupt, but college degrees are rarely revoked.

Superstars often say, "I have more than enough money, the house, the fine cars, but I still feel empty and lonely inside." This might be because THE TRUTH has confronted them, and they know there is very little substance and real talent within them. They may have been really lucky, or have capitalized on only one talent/skill, and they know if they lose that, they will have little to nothing else worthy of fame and fortune. Many celebrities who lose their popularity and marketability, have a difficult time maintaining healthy self-esteem.

People who get fired from employment need to be able to recover quickly. You can't spend a lot of time wallowing in self-pity. Honestly and diligently examine the circumstances of your termination. Even if it was your fault, admit it, and learn from your mistake. It's ok. We all make mistakes.

If you lose your job, but you know you have at least one strong set of skills {the more skills, the better (more than 10% of your brain)}, you will heal much better and faster. You will portray yourself much better in interviews.

People often say one solution for the poor in our economy is to provide jobs for those living in poverty and to have affordable housing for people living in poverty.

Jobs? … Really? There are plenty of jobs. There is no shortage of jobs. The job search websites list plenty of jobs every week.

The solution is getting people to qualify for the jobs. Affordable Housing?

The people need to have the skills and education to qualify for the jobs that give them adequate income to afford suitable housing.

It is a logical sequence of events. In high school, I attended a boarding school where the freshmen and seniors worked from 7:00 AM till noon and then attended classes from 1:00 PM till 5:00 PM. The sophomores and juniors attended classes from 7:00 AM till noon and worked from 1:00 PM till 5:00 PM. The money earned helped pay tuition at this private boarding school.

This practice could be the solution to our country's economy. Instead of under-educated adults and undocumented workers doing the labor (wage earners) and entry-level jobs, have our high school youth do these jobs. They will learn discipline, professional etiquette, and some can be promoted into supervisory positions to gain leadership skills. They can learn money management with their earnings. They can even save some of this money to pay for college.

Jobs for educated, skilled adult should be held by educated, skilled adults. These jobs give adults earning power to afford appropriate housing. If you are the head of your household, you should not work a minimum wage job.

The wages and salaries earned are a reflection of the time it takes to train for the job. Minimum wage jobs take [at most] a week to train to become competent at the job. High salaried jobs take years of formal education and months (usually three months-probation) of On-the-Job training to become competent the job. So, where do you want to spend the forty-five years, from high school graduation until retirement?

Every person should strive to be a self-supporting, independent adult. That means you should obtain the skills and education to acquire income (legally) through employment, entrepreneurship, or some creative/inventive manner to support yourself. Crabs in a barrel, in essence, are saying: "If I can't have it, neither can you." If I can't make progress, succeed and get out, I will become a weight on your back, and create difficulty and obstacles for you, so you can't get out either. Stay dumb and stupid like me so I won't feel so bad that I am dumb and stupid. Don't try for an advanced degree, so I won't feel bad that I didn't earn a degree. You think you're better than me?" Crabs will try to put you on a guilt trip for your accomplishments. Please don't show your intelligence or speak with an advanced vocabulary so I won't feel intimidated by you and so I can feel superior to you.

Can you see the ego? Can you see the compare and compete? Can you see the follower mentality? Stay down here in the bottom of the barrel, so we can all feel like we are a part of the crowd, content in our ignorance, not trying to make progress, or succeed at getting out.

Remember, most people only use 10% of their capabilities in their lifetime. Let's shoot for a passing grade of 80% or higher.

CHAPTER 6: It's Not an Adventure, It's Just a J-O-B

(Note: In this book, you will see many sentences, phrases, thoughts and messages repeated several times. This is intentional. Because we are so thoroughly indoctrinated, saturated, and inundated with the follower's way of thinking and the "old" way of doing things; ... new ideas, a new awareness, and the process of transitioning philosophies, thoughts, and lifestyle requires repetitive presentation.)

Just as your self-esteem should not be based on material possessions, your self-worth should not necessarily be based on your job or job title. Self-esteem and self-worth should be based on doing the best you can with what you've been given.

What did you do to make yourself worthy of your job?

People gain employment through many different means: formal education requirements, experience, good interviewing skills, nepotism, fraternization, default, volunteer, networking, inside connections, blackmail and so on. Often it is not the best or most qualified candidate selected to fill the open position.

What did you do to make yourself worthy of your job?

Do you have depth? Do you have more than one strong set of marketable skills? Did you spend your time wisely and learn everything you could possibly learn from that job? Did you take advantage of additional training and tuition assistance/reimbursement benefits?

If you did not do the things listed above, you

118

should start working on them now. If you feel trapped in a job, don't like your job, don't like your coworkers/boss, not making enough money to live independently, or debt-free, then make a step-by-step plan to change your life for the better.

This can be a short-term or long-term plan or both, whichever is appropriate, and whichever will work. The plan could be as simple as tightening up your résumé and distributing it on reputable employment websites. Or the plan could be as complicated as: move to a less expensive apartment or house, moving to a new city, build a savings account or investment portfolio, reducing your debt ratio, complete your degree, and earning an advanced degree, earning advanced certifications.

A "friend" hated her job, didn't get along with most of her co- workers, but she stayed there for six years because she was taking advantage of the tuition reimbursement. The fact that she was working on her long-term goal kept her motivated. She simply ignored the gossiping and taunting by her co-workers and kept her eyes on the prize.

You should have more than one plan. You can have many goals. And you should have contingency plans, "Plan B" and Plan "C" to be prepared for obstacles. And there will be obstacles. I encourage people to use the law of attraction but don't ever be so arrogant to think you control all circumstances surrounding you. Acknowledge a higher power. You can pray, but the answer may not be what you expected.

A radio personality said he never makes a Plan B because he always puts 100% of his efforts into his Plan A. He doesn't want to take away from his efforts on Plan A.

Remember, most people only use 10% of their brain's capability during their lifetime. You can do more than the ordinary. That's why there is a word in the dictionary called: extraordinary.

He was recommending working only one plan at a time. I don't recommend this because if something goes wrong with Plan A, you can already be close to completing or have already completed Plan B, and it can sustain you till you get back on track with Plan A. Don't sell yourself short, and don't leave yourself vulnerable or exposed to risk.

MANAGEMENT

Ninety percent of why the economy is in bad shape is due to poor management. Managers are on such a big ego trip, boosted by the job title, pay increase, and having authority over others. They forget about the intricate skills of leadership and motivating their subordinates to achieve the best performance and highest production possible.

Whenever I am being interviewed for a job, I ask, "What is your approach to problem- solving?"

If they don't say something like, "My first step in problem-solving is to properly identify the problem," I know this is not a good fit for me.

Whenever I am being interviewed for a job, I ask the inter- viewer, "What is your management style?" and "Do you micromanage?" Most of the time, the answer is, "No, I am not a micromanager." Once, the response was (very arrogantly); "If I have to micromanage you, then I don't need you here."

If a manager has the luxury to select her entire staff, she could select employees that are a good match for her management style. But the reality is most managers inherit most of their staff. Therefore, managers need to be versatile with their management styles.

The correct answer to the question, "What is your management style?" is, "I adjust my management style to fit the current issue or individual I am addressing at the time." The correct business term is "Situational Leadership" ®
www.situational.com

The manager's style should match the individual:

Manager Style: High Task/Low Relationship (Directing, Guiding, Telling) matches with Employee: Unable, Insecure, or Un-willing

Manager Style: High Task/High Relationship (Explaining, Selling, Encouraging) matches with Employee: Unable but Confident or Willing

Manager Style: High Relationship/Low Task (Persuading, Participating, Problem- Solving) matches with Employee: Able, but Insecure or Unwilling

Manager Style: Low Relationship/Low Task (Observing, Dele- gating, Monitoring) matches with Employee: Confident, Willing and Able.

Source: *"Situational Leadership"* ®
www.situational.com

New employees need to be micro-managed. Managers can say to the new employee, "I have read your résumé and I am aware of your skills and qualifications. I must let you know that you will be micromanaged for the first few months. It is my job to ensure that you acquire the training you need to succeed at this job. It may feel overbearing at times, but when I see you making the progress required, I will ease up."

If you are a new employee, make sure you learn all you need to know to succeed at your job. Your manager or trainer may have a hidden agenda and may feel threatened by you. Read your job description thoroughly and get a copy of the annual evaluation template. Know the criteria on which you will be rated and scored. Refer back to textbooks, order new books and stay current with professional journals in your field.

Obviously, not everyone is a Type A, nor do they want to be type A. Some trainers, coaches and managers have hidden agendas and motives. These Type As often speak at a rapid pace. This may or may not be an attempt to prevent their listener from receiving all information being presented. They can then check the box, indicating and date stamping that all necessary information was disseminated. Because their hidden motive is that they are impatient and resent non-type As. Their hidden agenda is to sabotage non- type As. They either pressure the employee into being type A or push them out.

If you are a manager, even your oldest and most experienced employees need micro- managing at times, maybe on a new project, maybe they are having a bad day, or feeling under the weather, or being distracted by personal issues. These things don't make them bad employees. They may just need some motivation and leadership or someone else to pick up the slack for a little while.

Managers should use evaluations as a learning and motivating tool. Don't waste time with irrelevant annotations. This will tear down morale and stunt motivation. Don't waste my time on an immaterial/De-minimis number of typing and spelling errors. It will tear down my morale and stunt my motivation.

So, my manager "wrote me up" on a quarterly performance evaluation and put it in my permanent record, each and every typing error and spelling error I made during the quarter. There were seven examples listed, out of 187 documents and emails of correspondence, during the specified time period. A month later, I had a "skip level" meeting with the territory manager, and I mentioned I felt like my manager was nit-picking at my work in pointing out each and every typing and spelling error within my work.

The territory manager proceeded to give me

suggestions on how to ensure my correspondence would be as error free as possible. For example, have a co-worker proofread my work before forwarding documents. I don't think he even considered that the manager might be unreasonable in documenting these errors, placing them in my permanent record and what affect this would have on my morale and motivation.

But that's par for the course for upper management automatically taking the side of middle management over the subordinate.

Once, I was marked poorly on technical/computer skills for having trouble with a faulty, "used" portable printer that had been issued to me. Within this same organization, another trainer was rude and impatient with me for asking how to perform a particular mathematical function. She had earlier emphasized that no question was a stupid question.

Although I may have learned this math in school, I had forgotten it at that time. Maybe I could understand her reaction if this were my third or fourth time asking, but it was my first time asking. She made negative reference to this situation in my performance evaluation.

Some managers want to be liked and to be friends with their subordinates. This is a dangerous slippery slope. The friendship and professionalism will eventually suffer because of the imbalance in power. Just avoid it. The same goes for parents "needing" to be liked and trying to be friends with their children. People say you must be respectful and show respect to your manager, as though it is a foregone or automatically required behavior. Contrary to popular belief, RESPECT IS EARNED over time. A subordinate is expected to show common courtesy, politeness and use the good manners their momma taught them. This is not necessarily RESPECT.

The difference is that an employee will be more agreeable to a manager's instructions, ideas, and proposals because, over time, the employee has come to see the manager's thought process, methods, and management style, which may or may not earn the respect of the employee. It takes time for the employee to observe the manager and form a working relationship with the manager.

This comes into play when a manager needs extra efforts, input, feedback, and extended hours from employees. An employee who wants to "brown nose" and "suck up" to the boss will only go so far if they are not receiving a pay-off. But if an employee truly respects a manager, they will not hesitate to go above and beyond the minimal requirements. An employee who does not truly respect their manager, will suck up, smile and brown nose to the boss's face, then gossip, undermine, and sabotage their boss behind their back.

People obtain management positions through many different circumstances: tenure, longevity, formal education requirements, experience, nepotism, fraternization, default, volunteer, blackmail and so on.

Many people who are selected as managers do not ever learn what it takes to be a good, productive, motivational manager. There is always room for improvement. There is always more to learn.

Some managers think they are "too cool" to study and use the traditional textbook tools for managers. These tools were included in textbook materials for a reason: They have been researched, and they work. I really like the concepts in "Situational Leadership" because it requires the manager to get to know the employees and customize their management style for that individual.

Some managers let being promoted to that position blow up their ego. And they never take the time to learn, then practice appropriate management skills.

Often subordinates are terminated because it was wrongfully determined the employee was incompetent, but the truth was the manager did not have the skills or patience to motivate and bring the best out of that individual. That is what management is supposed to be all about.

Managers tend to be impatient, sarcastic, and cruel to poor performers. The poor performers are the employees who need the managers the most. The highly rated, highly motivated employees don't need management and supervision as much, do they.

Yes, there are standards, deadlines, and required production levels, and the manager is responsible for meeting these or- organizational objectives. Therefore, they must weigh the cost and benefit, cause and effect, pros and cons, of terminating an employee, paying severance, paying unemployment and other benefits to the terminated individual. Then there's the workload during the gap time between the old and new team member and then interviewing, hiring, training, and providing benefits to a replacement employee. And you must consider the morale and loyalty of the remaining individuals. It is possible it would be better to use proven management tactics and tools to bring each team member up to standards rather than firing them.

Far too few companies require the employees to evaluate the managers' performance during the annual performance review process. These evaluations should go both ways. The assessment given by the subordinates may not carry the same weight, but each team member's opinions should definitely be considered, evaluated for validity and truthfulness. You may also choose to keep the management evaluations confidential and anonymous. Many times, upper management abruptly dismisses the opinions, observations and complaints of subordinate employees, with no regard, and automatically take the word of the immediate supervisor. Remember, there are ALWAYS at least two sides to every story.

At orientation, a division leader stressed that "your reputation will precede you wherever you go. Try to maintain a good reputation." He really stressed this, … strongly, … repeatedly.

This is good AND BAD advice.

I ascertained that gossiping was a very strong and supported part of this organization's corporate culture, which is a bad thing.

I humbly suggest that you approach each person on an individual basis. Give them a clean slate with which to start. Don't pre-judge a person by rumors and reputation. Just because one person had a good experience with an individual doesn't mean the next person will. Just because one person had a bad experience with an individual doesn't mean the next person will.

You don't know who is at fault for the bad experience. There are always at least two sides to every story. You can try really hard and work diligently to earn and maintain a good reputation, but some things are beyond your control, and you can never please all the people all the time.

People get in their office clique and gossip groups and wallow and fester in negativity toward an individual. Then they spread this wrong information with new employees, trying to recruit others and strengthen the alliance against the outcast individual.

If you are a new employee, be very careful about joining office cliques and gossip groups. It is a very slippery slope and a double-edged sword. Some people never graduate from the gossip groups, popular cliques, and immature mentality when they leave high school.

"When I was a child, I talked like a child, I thought like a child, and reasoned like a child. When I became a man, I put childish ways behind me."

1 Corinthians 13:11

(Note: There is a chapter in this book dedicated to examining the dynamics and nuances of gossip}

CHAPTER SEVEN: THE FIRST STEP IS TO IDENTIFY THE PROBLEM: PROBLEM-SOLVING PROPERLY

Problem Solving 101:

1. Properly identify the problem.

2. List seven to ten possible realistic solutions.

3. Test your list of solutions. List possible realistic results of each solution.

4. Select the best solution.

5. Implement the solution.

6. Follow-up and evaluate the solution.

You can't skip the first step. If you do not have an ulterior motive, a hidden agenda, or if you are not in denial or intentionally trying to let time run out, you must take the time to identify the problem correctly.

If you don't properly identify the real, true problem, the solution you choose will not solve the actual problem, and the problem will continue to exist or will return at a future date. Don't be intimidated by the list of problem- solving techniques.

Start slow and take it step by step. As with any skill that you repeat and practice, you will improve over time. You will become confident and competent as you master your problem- solving skills.

Keep your ego out of your problem-solving process. A person often knows the best solution, but they may want to "save face." They may be worried about other people's opinions. Some problems are more complex than others. Have you heard the saying, "Inch by inch anything is a cinch?" If you analyze as many relevant contributing factors as time will allow (take the time, make the time), and list them in a logical order, then you can, step by step, create a map from the starting point of the problem to the destination of the solution.

Some methods relate more to business practices than to personal life situations. In some cases, it will be obvious which method is best, and in other situations, you may have to try more than one method to see which is optimal.

Use your computer to research: Problem Solving Techniques.

Problem-solving methods and techniques: Cash Flow Fore- casts, Cause and Effect Diagrams, Flow Charts, PEST Analysis, Porter's Five Forces, Risk Analysis, SWOT (Strengths, Weaknesses, Opportunities, Threats), Systems Diagrams, USP Analysis, and Value Chain. You can go to any search engine and find an abundance of information on each of these methods.

Problem-solving is a skill that can be practiced, sharpened and mastered!

The McKinsey Mind *Understanding and Implementing the Problem-Solving Tools and Management Techniques of the World's Top Strategic Consulting Firm* by Ethan Rasiel and PhD, Paul N. Friga (Hardcover - Sep 26, 2001)

CHAPTER 8:

Pick One, Any One, Hurry Up and Decision Make

Decision making skills should be your top priority for learning and mastering. They determine everyone's success in both professional and private life.

I find it concerning when a woman cannot make a decision, because she has been programmed not to. (Please Read Chapter 12 – twice!) Unfortunately, and erroneously, she has bought into the LIE that she is intellectually inferior to men and the LIE that she should let men make decisions for her.

Just as with problem-solving skills, decision-making is a skill that can be practiced, sharpened and mastered!

The key is very simple: TAKE THE TIME to analyze your options. Whichever method you choose, TAKE THE TIME to analyze your options and opportunities.

Go to:
https://www.mindtools.com/pages/main/new MN_TED.htm

PART 3:

RELATING ...TOO PERSONAL

CHAPTER NINE

THANKS MOM! NOW HOW MUCH DO I OWE YOU!

Emotional Blackmail

(Note: In this book, you will see many sentences, phrases, thoughts, and messages repeated several times. This is intentional. Because we are so thoroughly indoctrinated and thoroughly saturated with the follower's way of thinking and the "old" way of doing things; new ideas, a new awareness and the process of transitioning philosophies, thoughts, and lifestyle requires repetitive presentation.)

Unplanned and Unwanted Pregnancies

Followers think it is ok and it's not a big deal to have un-planned or unwanted pregnancies because it happens so often to so many people. Followers think un-planned or unwanted pregnancies are acceptable and part of the "norm."

(Unwanted: meaning undesired by either or both parents)

Having a child is an extremely serious commitment. This commitment is irrevocably binding for mature, responsible people of substance. Check the statistics on the percent of single-parent families in the 1960s, the 1980s, and 2000s.

https://www.census.gov/data/tables/time-series/demo/families/families.html

Are we becoming a nation of accidents? What are the implications? What are the consequences? What kind of future can we expect?

Let me ask you something, How old were you when you learned from where babies come?

Let's take our intelligence, maturity, and discipline to the next level.

Most people are followers. Most people only use 10% of their brain capabilities during their lifetime. Try using more.

Can you afford to raise your child/children properly, pay for a quality education (past high school), spend quality time, help them with their homework, get to know their teachers, teach them manners, teach them to speak correctly, teach them to respect themselves, and teach them to be polite and courteous?

Some single adults can afford to have children, and some cannot.

Some ignorant people have children and don't have the knowledge base and intelligence that they should have in order to teach and pass correct information on to their children. So then, the children never learn the basic essentials for a productive, fulfilling life. And each generation descends further and further into an ignorant state of being.

Then those who dare to speak the truth about this vicious downward spiral from intelligence to stupidity are scorned and called self-haters or racist.

"Crabs in a barrel" not carrying their own weight, literally draining resources and forcing others to take care of them.

Every person should be self-sufficient. And when

they have children, one of their parental responsibilities is to teach their children to be self-sufficient.

A friend told me her husband was pressuring her into having a second child. She didn't want a second child at that time, partly because they had both just started paying back student loans. They were struggling with finances and other marital issues. Her mother had told her, "Never have more children than you can afford to take care of alone, even if you have a husband." In most cases, the ultimate responsibility of the children falls upon the mother.

But first, ask yourself, can you afford to take care of yourself without draining resources from others? Do you have employment, bringing in enough income to provide for your housing, food, and clothing? Independently?

If you can't even afford to take care of yourself, how can you bring a child into the world and expect to take care of you and your child? Does the child's father (to be) have employment, bringing in enough income to provide for his own housing, food, and clothing? Here are some resources to help you determine:

www.bankrate.com/calculat ors/savings/raise-child- calculator.aspx

Child Affordability Calculator - Calculate the costs of raising a child | Planswell

Child Cost Calculator (csgnetwork.com)

If your plan is to drain resources from family members (parents and siblings) welfare, or government agencies, just re-state the meaning and say, "I am irresponsible, I used extremely poor judgment and did not take very easy, very reasonable, very inexpensive steps to prevent pregnancy and had a child I could not afford. I will be draining scarce resources from my family, not contributing to the prosperity of my family and my race, but draining from my family and my race, and feeding into the negative stereotypes of my family and my race."

Don't give me that deer in the headlights look, as if it was beyond your control, as if ignorance is your "valid excuse." How old were you when you learned from where babies come?

Sometimes we hear people speak as though pregnancy is some kind of INVOLUNTARY, miraculous, immaculate conception, without knowledge, conscious decision or passive decision that unprotected sexual intercourse will create a pregnancy.

You hear something like, "We were messing around, off and on, for months, and low & behold, and then I came up pregnant."

Having children is a very serious life-long commitment.

Having a child is not the meaning of life. For some, it is the element that gives their life the most meaning, but having a child is not the meaning of life.

Use more than 10% of your capabilities. Ten percent is such a small fraction. Explore your artistic talents, sing, dance, paint, write a book! Take a physical challenge, train and run a marathon, take classes and develop a second or third set of marketable skills. Become debt free, build savings and investments, become a mentor, discover the cure for terminal diseases, or build a better mousetrap. Be good to yourself. Find your personal best.

Having children is a very serious, life-long commitment. But first, consider the commitment with the other parent-to-be. Is that person committed to you and your relationship? If not, has this person demonstrated they can set and reach a long-term goal? Can they focus and commit to anything? Why would you have a child (***which is a long-term commitment***) with a person who can't commit?

Just as we advise people who have recently gone through a break-up, "You need to work on yourself, do some introspection, before entering into another relationship." Before becoming a parent, you need to work on yourself and do some introspection.

Do you have the patience to interact with a toddler, an adolescent, a teenager?

Ladies: are you comparing and competing with your teenage daughter?

Are you jealous of her youth, beauty, and intelligence?

Is she out-achieving you, when you were her age, or currently?

Having unwanted or unplanned children is a form of the "crabs in a barrel" syndrome. You will be pulling someone else down, pulling from someone else's resources and funds to support you and your child. You will drain resources from family, friends, or government resources.

It is great that the government has safety nets and programs for people who accidentally make mistakes and occasionally fall on hard times, as opposed to people who have a lifestyle and an entire lifetime of poor choices and poor decisions.

What if the government could drastically cut down on that program and put that money into raising teacher salaries and better elementary and high school programs?

A person's sanity is directly proportionate with their ability to comprehend and accept the truth.

The truth is not always pleasant or nice.

Stop trying to sugarcoat the truth. Not all children are a blessing. Some pregnancies/children are a huge, gigantic mistake that couldn't have happened at a worse time.

Now I know some people rise to the challenge, and some even rise well above the challenge. But why not avoid the difficulty, to begin with?

Not every person is meant to reproduce. Look how many children are in the foster care system. Having children is not the meaning of life. Stop wallowing in the follower mentality.

I was speaking to a friend who had been dating a guy for about six months. She sounded extremely excited and happy. I asked her why? She said this guy told her he wanted her to have his baby.

My next question was: What are your feelings for him? Honestly? Then, Are you in love with him after six months? What are his feelings for you? Is he in love with you? What are his and your feelings about a long-term commitment to each other?

Have you heard about these people who use hook-up websites (as opposed to dating websites) for co-parenting without a commitment to each other?

HOW TWISTED!!!

What a great responsibility to bring a soul, a spirit, to fruition. The two of you conjured a soul incarnate. It is your responsibility to bring it to enlightenment and prepare it for the journey to nirvana.

Don't take this responsibility lightly. Don't minimize "THE TRUTH" with your 10% follower mentality.

What a great responsibility to birth a child into the world. It is your job, your obligation to society and the entire planet, to raise this child to make a positive contribution to the world.

Metaphysically speaking: the benefits and creativity/manifestation powers grow exponentially for a sound, healthy, solid, committed couple.

Family dynamics matter!

Physical Abuse of a Child

There is a difference between appropriate discipline and abuse.

If you don't already have children and you are contemplating becoming a parent, please consider if you will have the time and patience to raise your children properly. Patience is crucial.

The abuse stems from the abuser's weak self- esteem and their ego's twisted need to degrade, overpower or control another person. If your self-esteem is based on the right thing, you will not feel the need to degrade, overpower, or control another person to boost your ego.

It happens in the best of families, and it happens in the worst of families.

Physical abuse is erroneously used as a control mechanism in some families, where maintaining appearances and social status is made a high priority.

In some families, mounting financial debt, feelings of inadequacies, and other associated stresses push a person to abuse to gain ego points by degrading or overpowering another person.

Sometimes a person who was abused becomes an abuser. Because of feelings of embarrassment, anger, frustration, confusion (not understanding why the abuse occurred), feeling helpless to prevent it, a person who has been abused chooses to abuse another person to gain feelings of empowerment and control. The newly abused person has a twisted need to degrade someone else to make themselves feel better about themselves.

If you are a child abuser or have anger management issues, go and get professional help. You can get help from social service agencies, the church, support groups, therapists, and psychiatrists.

MENTAL ABUSE and NEGLECT OF A CHILD

Before entering into the commitment of having a child, consider and estimate if you will have enough time to devote ad equate quality time with your child (nurturing, helping with homework, entertainment, visiting with teachers, coaching, and attending sports events).

Consider if you would have to work two or three jobs to support your child. Consider if your career demands too much of your time, with extended office hours and traveling.

The brain craves stimulation through challenges and learning. If you do not fulfill this craving with positive, constructive activities, the default will be stagnate, or negative, and destructive. Spend quality time with your child regularly.

If your self-esteem is based on the right thing, you won't need to degrade, belittle, and cause your child mental anguish for the purpose of boosting your own ego.

Using children as Leverage in Divorce or Separation: Hurting someone else to gain ego bonus points is wrong. Your children realize (or will eventually realize) what you are doing. They will lose respect for you. They may even grow to hate you.

When a couple breaks up, it hurts. When children are involved, it gets complicated. That's why you should consider the commitment to each other BEFORE you bring children into the situation.

A person's sanity is directly proportionate with their ability to comprehend and accept the truth.

Can you accept the truth if there is no more romantic, loving relationship between you and your child's other parent? You need to face the facts and accept the truth.

Fill your life and your child's life with educational and creative challenges.

CREATING A MOMMA'S BOY

Being a good mother/parent is truly an important responsibility.

Suppose you took advantage of all the educational opportunities and you took advantage of career opportunities and are independent and self-sufficient. In that case, your self-esteem should be based on the fact that you can honestly say, "I did the best I could with the opportunities I was given."

It is wrong to create a child who is emotionally dependent on you, meaning they can't decide without asking your opinion and gaining your approval first.

Making your child feel guilty if they don't stroke your ego and praise you is wrong. Waiting on your child "Hand & Foot", cooking and cleaning for them, past the age of seventeen, not teaching them to do these things for themselves, and your motive is to keep them dependent on you, to stroke your own ego and make you feel important, is wrong.

Some women do these things because their self-worth is based on the wrong thing.

It is nice to have a loving family. It feels good to have your children's love and respect. Therefore, make yourself worthy of love and   respect.   Don't

guilt,   cripple {emotionally or financially},
blackmail your children into "faking" that they love
and respect you.

If you are not worthy of love and respect and you
have not truly earned their respect, the behavior they
show toward you will be fake (all or in part).

This brings to mind: mothers-in-law who compete with
daughters-in-law for their son's attention and financial
support. If a man is a "Momma's Boy" and he cannot
keep his mother an appropriate, acceptable,
comfortable distance from your relationship, you need
to run, not walk away.

CHAPTER TEN:

IS THAT A FACT JACK, OR IS THAT JUST YOUR OPINION?

(Note: In this book, you will see many sentences, phrases, thoughts, and messages repeated several times. This is intentional. Because we are so thoroughly indoctrinated and thoroughly saturated with the follower's way of thinking and the "old" way of doing things; new ideas, a new awareness and the process of transitioning philosophies, thoughts and lifestyles require a repetitive presentation.)

"Followers" also base their self-worth, all or in part, on other people's opinions. This plays itself out when the follower intentionally tries to make others jealous by showing off, bragging and getting mad when someone says something bad about the follower.

This kind of person has the problematic "need to be liked," and the need for likes and followers on social media, a people pleaser, a yes man/person, parents trying to be friends with their young children, managers needing to be friends and liked by their subordinates.

Be very careful with "Other People's Opinions." Do not base your self-worth (not even in part) on other people's opinion. I am not saying don't listen to other's opinions or constructive criticism. Remember, most people only use 10% of their brain capability during a lifetime.

THERE IS ALWAYS SOMETHING ELSE TO LEARN!

THERE IS ALWAYS ROOM FOR

IMPROVEMENT!

There is a popular saying, "Opinions are like ass holes; every-BODY has one." But there are certain elements that make one opinion more significant than another. Is this opinion based on facts or pre-judged (prejudiced) assumptions?

In medical situations, you may ask a second doctor for a second opinion. You wouldn't ask an accountant for a second opinion about a medical condition. Why wouldn't you? Because some people are better qualified to render a relevant, educated opinion on a particular subject matter than others.

When contemplating other people's opinions, consider the source and consider the motivation. Ask yourself; is the opinion based on FACTS? Is this opinion based on popular opinion (following the crowd)? Is this opinion based on gut feeling or intuition? Is the opinion RELEVANT? What difference does this opinion make to my life, health, and progress? Is this person trying to control me or manipulate me with their opinion?

Whether the opinion comes from your worst enemy or a stranger on the street, if the FACTS are valid and relevant to your life, health, and progress, you should listen to the opinion.

KNOWLEDGE IS INFINITE

THERE IS ALWAYS MORE TO KNOW. THERE IS ALWAYS ROOM TO GROW.

Don't be hurt by someone else's opinion. Humans are

not perfect. EXAMINE THE FACTS. If you need to change, then make a step-by-step plan to change.

Often in defensive situations, you hear people say: "Don't judge me," or "You have no right to judge me," or "Don't be so judgmental," or even "You are very opinionated."

Go to the dictionary and look up the words: judge and opinion. They are synonyms.

In verb form, one meaning of judge is to form an opinion of; decide upon critically.

The noun form of opinion means a belief, or judgment, or estimate.

Everyone is entitled to their own opinion of others, and therefore, everyone is entitled to their own judgment of others.

Consequently, people with the follower mentality think, for some reason, we don't have the right to judge one another. When, in fact, we do.

Using the phrase, "You have no right to judge me" is an invalid defense mechanism and a defensive distraction.

Anyone can observe a situation, gather, then analyze related facts and form a judgment or opinion. The words opinion and judgement are synonymous.

Here is further proof.

Many judicial courts are ruled by judicial panels (for example, the U.S. Supreme Court has a panel of nine judges). Each conclusion of the trial renders a judgment. Each judgement renders a majority OPINION and a dissenting OPINION.

By definition, the majority opinion is a judicial opinion agreed upon by more than half of the members of a court. A majority opinion sets forth the judgement of the court and an explanation of the rationale behind the court's judgement.

By definition, the dissenting opinion (or dissent) is an opinion in a legal case, in certain legal systems, written by one or more judges expressing disagreement with the court's majority opinion.

The semantics of the situation are that the majority opinion becomes (or changes its title to) the judgement. In courts where there is only one judge, their observations and analysis of the facts becomes the majority opinion (an opinion of one) and thus the judgement.

The words opinion and judgement are synonymous.

At this point, some people like to bring up the Bible verse: Matthew 7:1 Judge not, lest ye be judged.

But what about verse 2: For, in the same way you judge others, you will be judged, and with the same measure you use, it will be measured to you.

To me, this is saying; everyone develops an opinion on everything; whether they express it verbally or not, they have an opinion. Therefore, everyone has passed judgement on you; whether they express it verbally or not, they have passed judgement. Now, if you are assuming the worst about others, without supporting facts, and you are spreading false gossip, invalid opinions, unsubstantiated judgements, lies and rumors, with the intent of causing adversity, it will all come right back around to you.

Matthew 7: 2 For in the same way you judge others, you will be judged, and with the measure you use, it will be measured to you.

Judgements or opinions will be formulated no matter the situation, by all people, at all times. You can play with the words to soothe your ego, but this will only be a temporary fix.

Properly identify the problem.

Is the problem: one person expressing a judgment or opinion about another person? Is the problem that a person's feelings are hurt [or more accurately put: someone's EGO is hurt] because one person expresses a judgment or opinion about another person? Is that the problem? Is the problem that a person's self-esteem is partially based on other people's opinions or approval?

Your self-esteem, nor your EGO, should be based on other people's opinions.

Your self-esteem should be based on doing the best you can with what you've been given.

Examine the opinion for facts, then disregard the rest. If the facts indicate you need to change, then begin to work on changing and disregard the rest.

I have many friends, colleagues, and family

members whose opinions I value. I seek their opinions and advise on a regular basis. I respect their philosophies, chain of logic, and analytical thought processes, which produce sound, fact-based opinions as opposed to following the crowd, trends, or whimsical, ego-driven frivolity.

I value and cherish my mother's opinions, but I do not base my self-esteem on her opinions. We disagree on many things. We even have opposite opinions on some of my lifestyle choices. We are mature enough and loving enough to peacefully agree to disagree. This is not an ego race. There is no competition to see who can control whom, or who can manipulate whom, score more points, or (quote): "win" the disagreement.

I love and cherish my mother, but I do not base my self-esteem or self-worth on her opinion. I would never do anything to intentionally hurt or embarrass her or cause her any stress or pain.

But I do realize that for other people, not all mothers are as thoughtful, loving, caring, kind and ego-less as my mother.

(Note: there is another chapter in this book that discusses using people as emotional crutches, co-dependency, and enablers of toxic behavior and another chapter on emotional blackmailers)

Often, we see celebrities lash out or "clap back" at other people who express an adverse opinion about the celebrity. The ego is the most significant problem celebrities have on so many different levels and dimensions.

I have heard of people trying desperately to gain

another person's approval, usually a child trying to gain the approval of their mother or father. Well, usually, until a child reaches adulthood, the child has to follow the advice given by the parents (unless it is illegal).

But sometimes, this carries over into adulthood, and the mother or father is still trying to control the child with emotional blackmail. As an adult, you can listen to the advice/opinions of your parents but examine the advice/opinion for factuality and relevance, then develop and use your own decision- making and problem-solving skills.

There are college courses, business school classes, self-enrichment classes, books and literature on how to develop decision- making and problem-solving skills.

Don't let another person manipulate you or control you with their opinions.

I have heard of people who don't want to work out at health clubs because they are afraid of what others might think or say. STOP WORRYING ABOUT THE OTHER PEOPLE AT THE HEALTH CLUBS. First of all, are they people you know? Do you actually know their name? Do you, in fact, know their personalities? Have you had more than a five-minute conversation with them?

You should be there for your own personal health/fitness goals - NOT TO COMPARE AND COMPETE WITH THE OTHER PEOPLEIN THE GYM FOR EGO BONUS POINTS!

[Note: We will discuss self-image and the ties between physical and mental health in another chapter in this book.]

Are you afraid that some people will snicker, laugh, and point at you when you walk into the gym? People, most of whom you don't even know.

But if they are snickering and pointing, maybe you need to check yourself. Or perhaps they are just immature simpletons who you should ignore anyway.

People say they don't want to go to a particular nightclub because the people act snobby there.

What does their behavior have to do with your personal reasons for going to a nightclub?

Unless the other people in the club are threatening bodily harm, the snobby behavior should be ignored.

Repeat ten times:

1. You are entitled to your own opinion. My self-esteem is not even in the smallest fraction, based on your opinion.

2. You are entitled to your own opinion. My self-esteem is not even in the smallest fraction, based on your opinion.

3.   You are entitled to your own opinion. My self-esteem is not even in the smallest fraction, based on your opinion.

4.   You are entitled to your own opinion. My self-esteem is not even in the smallest fraction, based on your opinion.

5.   You are entitled to your own opinion. My self-esteem is not even in the smallest fraction, based on your opinion.

6.   You are entitled to your own opinion. My self-esteem is not even in the smallest fraction, based on your opinion.

7.   You are entitled to your own opinion. My self-esteem is not even in the smallest fraction, based on your opinion.

8.   You are entitled to your own opinion. My self-esteem is not even in the smallest fraction, based on your opinion.

9.   You are entitled to your own opinion. My self-esteem is not even in the smallest fraction, based on your opinion.

10.   You are entitled to your own opinion. My self-esteem is not even in the smallest fraction, based on your opinion.

There will always be petty, negative, immature, jealous people you will encounter from time to time and place to place, so when someone gives their opinion or criticizes you, examine it for factuality, accept what is truthful, and disregard the rest.

Are you going to the club with your friend(s) for your own personal reasons, for example, to hang out, to celebrate, to dance, to literally: raise your vibration and frequency?

It is truly unnecessary to be influenced by the opinions of others - most of whom you don't even know.

There was a "judge" character on the tv show *The Good Wife* in her courtroom, during court, she would make each lawyer and each witness say "in my opinion" after every paragraph spoken. At first, you (as the viewer of the show) and the char- acters within the show became annoyed by this constant repeating of this phrase. It would seem obvious that the words that come out of an individual's mouth are their own opinions.

But it is not always apparent or understood by the speaker or the listener that the words spoken are **only the speaker's opinion**, observations, and analysis of surrounding, contributing factors.

Often, the speaker (because of ego) thinks their opinion is "the law," "the Gospel," the only point of view that should matter, when, in fact, their opinion may not carry any more significance or importance than anyone else's. We should all develop and sharpen our analytical skills and critical thinking abilities so that we can recognize opinions as opinions. Separate facts and significant items, use analysis and come to a logical conclusion … which is still … just your opinion.

But you can then say: "My opinion is based on Fact #1_____Fact #2_____Fact #3 _____… and so on.

Some people can NOT get their egos out of the way long enough to say and truly accept: to agree to disagree. To these people, each discussion and debate must end in persuading one person to abandon their own opinion and adopt the opinion of their opponent, therefore rendering a "W" or an "L." Some people are always in a compare and compete state of mind.

Repeat ten times:

1.   You are entitled to your own opinion, and we can agree to disagree.

2. You are entitled to your own opinion, and we can agree to disagree.

3. You are entitled to your own opinion, and we can agree to disagree.

4. You are entitled to your own opinion, and we can agree to disagree.

5. You are entitled to your own opinion, and we can agree to disagree.

6. You are entitled to your own opinion, and we can agree to disagree.

7. You are entitled to your own opinion, and we can agree to disagree.

8. You are entitled to your own opinion, and we can agree to disagree.

9. You are entitled to your own opinion, and we can agree to disagree.

10. You are entitled to your own opinion, and we can agree to disagree.

The serenity prayer:

"Lord, help me to change the things I can, to accept the things I cannot change and grant me the wisdom to know the difference."

There will always be petty, negative, jealous people. You cannot change that, so when someone gives their opinion/criticizes you, examine it for factuality, accept what is truthful, and disregard the rest.

I used to have a coworker who hated my guts, and I really, genuinely don't know why. I have my suspicions. But she was so tightly wound up with hatred for me, we couldn't have a mature, civil conversation on the topic.

Whenever someone was gossiping and speaking badly about me, she was always ready to enthusiastically jump in, embellish, instigate, and add her hate- spewing comments. In contrast, if someone were saying something good about me, complimenting me, or speaking about my awards and accomplishments, she would literally hiss, then tried to pivot or stop the conversation, or she would simply ignore it or pretend she didn't hear any of the nice things said about me.

People often have selective hearing, selective comprehension, and selective memory.

Selective Hearing: Some people hear only what they want to hear. Some people twist the meaning of something they heard spoken verbally into what they want it to mean. Some people arrogantly, yet erroneously assume they know the speaker's intention and what the speaker meant to say (reading between the lines.)

Selective Comprehension: Some people extend compassion and understanding to some but not to others. Some people are willing to put a great deal of effort into understanding a situation or explanation for some individuals and not so much for others.

Selective Memory: Some people choose to remember names, situations, comments, explanations and stories from some, but not from others.

If someone WANTS to feel bad about you or think poorly of you, they will find anything (fabricated or factual) to support what they WANT to feel. They will choose to ignore anything-fabricated or factual - in opposition to what they WANT to feel.

Unfortunately, some people have the distorted need to degrade or belittle another person to make them feel better about themselves.

CHILDHOOD BULLYING:

To the bully: If your self-esteem is based on the right thing, you won't need to degrade others to make yourself feel better about yourself. Parents should teach children that self-worth and self-esteem should be based on "Doing the best you can with what you've been given," not on a superficial or self- created sense of superiority. Self-esteem should not be based on compare and compete, and not on being in the popular clique.

It may be difficult for young, immature minds to comprehend. Adults might start by asking the child: "How would you feel if others were pointing and laughing at you?" Also, point out that what goes around comes around. When you are mean to other people, mean things come back to you. When you are good to other people, good things will come back to you. Tell them, "I know you are a child, you should be allowed to enjoy your childhood and have fun, but there are certain situations where every person, young or old, should behave in a kind, courteous, and mature manner.

Involve your child in many activities to keep them occupied and challenged. The brain craves activity and learning. If we don't actively provide positive and progressive input, the default is negativity and destruction. You've heard the saying: "The idle mind is the playground of the devil." Help children set short term goals. Work with them to make a step-by-step plan to reach their goal. Encourage them and reward them when they reach their goals.

To the child being bullied: short of physical abuse, everything else should be ignored. You've heard the saying: "Sticks and stones may break my bones, but names will never hurt me." Your self-worth should not be based on other people's opinion. Name calling, teasing and taunting should be ignored.

I know this is easier said than done. Children want to fit in and have many friends. Explain to your child that as you go through life, there will always be some people who like you, and there will always be some people who don't like you – and that's ok, that's just a part of real life, and it's ok, nothing to get upset about. You will never get 100% of people to like you or agree with you.

Further, explain: Some people have a sick need to degrade others to make themselves feel better about themselves. Understand that what goes around; comes around. If you spread negativity and hate – you will receive negativity and hate in return. **If you spread love and positivity, you will receive love and positivity back.**

Also, explain: the bully is looking for a particular reaction from you; they are looking for you to break down, cry, show fear or cower. The bully is looking to feed their ego with the negative energy created within the person they are bullying. If they don't get the reaction they are looking for, they will likely give up. If they can't feed their ego at your table, they will have to go some where else if they want to get fed.

Of course, physical abuse should be reported, and self-defense is an appropriate reaction.

****

Social   Media,   Pop   Culture, Celebrity, Followers, and Likes

Facebook creators knew exactly what they were doing when they created the platform. A prior creation of Mr. Z was a website that compared females' photos to each other to see who would get a higher score. The site also compared female's photos to animals. The operative word being compared. Most people use compare and compete to determine their self-esteem and self-worth.

Facebook is a platform perfectly designed for compare and compete. Some people compare their appearance, accomplishments, possessions, vacations, the number of followers, and the number of likes, all in an attempt to gain ego bonus points.

People base their self-esteem (even a small part) on other people's opinions get an ego boost and, in fact, an adrenaline boost from receiving "Likes," subscribers and followers. But did you know that the owners, operators, and custodians of social media platforms manipulate the receipt and timing of responses (likes)? If you don't have your self-esteem and self-worth based on the right thing, you will be swayed and become a slave to social media.

I remember when cell phones first came out and became a common purchase/possession. It was like a status symbol to have a car phone and, soon after that, a handheld cell phone. It became an ego boost to show off, brag and boast about your cell phone.

People wanted to talk all the time on the cell phones, to look important or seem like: "I'm so important and needed that I must be reachable at all times." Do you remember pagers? I have seen adults who can't pay their rent [not mortgage] living with their parents, yet they insist on having the latest, most expensive version of the smartphone.

Of course, there are people and circumstances where communication is absolutely imperative, but we know and recognize those people who are addicted to their electronic devices. These insecure people have a constant need for compare & compete, a constant need for validation and corroboration, and a constant need for attention.

If you have your self-esteem based on the right thing, you will not require these superficial, external items or acts to fill a void. I keep reiterating that it is an internal thing, not an external thing.

Understand that you are human, and you are not perfect. You should not base your self- esteem on other people's opinions (not even the smallest fraction of it). You should not be wounded or hurt because someone is critical of you or disagrees with you. Search the criticism for the truth. If the truth is that you need to make corrections or change something, then make a plan and take the steps to change.

But always remember, you will never please all of the people all of the time; meaning, there will always be someone who is displeased with you, and there will always be someone who disagrees with you. If you don't base your self- esteem on other people's opinions, you won't be hurt when displeasure and disagreement occur. This is where you say: "You are certainly entitled to your own opinion" and "We can agree to disagree." To earn ego bonus points, some immature followers consistently quantify every situation as a "W" or an "L," a win or a loss. You will never get everyone to agree with you. Some people have an adverse reaction when faced with disagreement. They think of it as a loss. A disagreement is not necessarily a loss. But some people can't get their heads out of the compare and compete, so to them, and everything ends in a "W" or an "L."

There is a popular motivational speaker who talks about being vulnerable. I have a great deal of respect for her, and I know she has helped many people, but I disagree with the concept of vulnerability. If you recognize the difference between ego and self-esteem, and you have your self-esteem based on the right thing, you will also recognize that it is more likely that your ego is vulnerable to being hurt rather than your self-es- teem. (go back and read chapter One)

If your ego is minimized and under control, your ego will only be minimally bruised. Therefore, you, yourself and your self-esteem are not vulnerable. You are not your ego. But if your ego is over-inflated and your ego is actually in control of you, then you will be overly sensitive and defensive whenever criticized.

You nor your self-esteem, doesn't have to be vulnerable or at risk of being bruised. Get rid of that "need to be liked." Really, its your ego that needs to be liked.

It is good to be friendly, kind, and courteous.

But if someone does not like you for who you truly are (not the fake, the brown-nosing you), then move on to people who do like the real you and with whom you are compatible.

THE FIRST STEP IS TO PROPERLY IDENTIFY THE PROBLEM.

It is so pathetic when celebrities react poorly when they receive criticism through social media or other sources. THE PROPERLY IDENTIFIED PROBLEM is that celebrities are often run by their egos and not the other way around. That is usually why they seek celebrity, in the first place: their ego. They want as many followers, subscribers and "likes" as they can get. The more they get, the more their egos grow. Celebrities should repeat several times out loud, they are entitled to their own opinion, and my self-esteem is not even in the smallest fraction, based on their opinion.

If your art is to bring a script for a play or a movie to life, you might be satisfied working with your local theatre company or creating independent movies. Check the true motivation. Does your ego feed off cheering crowds, many admiring eyes on you, people clambering and chaos trying to get to you? Do you want the biggest house in Beverly hills?

How much money is enough? Are you comparing and competing to have the biggest and baddest material possessions and to make others jealous? Properly identify the problem. Check your true motives.

… speaking of other people's opinions …
Some people are acting as though recognizing that someone has Selective Outrage is intellectually, philosophically and analytically advanced, or that someone that practices Selective Outrage is not intellectually, philosophically or analytically astute.

Have you heard the saying "Chose your battles wisely"? Of course, everyone should be selective with what and whom they allow to push them to outrage. Scenarios which evoke outrage should be scarce and few. Should we be outraged by every single incident or disagreement? Absolutely not. Success is 10% of what happens to you and 90% of how you react to it.

Spiritually and metaphysically, being low to anger or avoiding anger all together is the best route to take. You don't want to generate negative energy within and around you, which will attract more negative energy within and around you.

People who are controlled by their ego spend the majority of their time defensive and thin sinned.

CHAPTER 11: Be My Emotional Crutch, and I'll Lean on You Forever and Ever, and Ever Ever?   The Art of Co-Dependency

(Note: In this book, you will see many sentences, phrases, thoughts, and messages repeated several times. This is intentional. Because we are so indoctrinated and thoroughly saturated with the follower's way of thinking and the "old" way of doing things;   new ideas, a new awareness and the process of transitioning philosophies, thoughts, and lifestyles, requires a repetitive presentation.)

THE TRUTH AND REALITY WILL CONFRONT YOU SOONER OR LATER, PERIODICALLY, OCCASIONALLY OR OFTEN. YOU CAN COUNT ON THAT.

A person's sanity is directly proportionate with their ability to comprehend and accept the truth.

If you are lying to yourself, if you are in denial, refusing to accept the truth. Your lies are your emotional crutch.

PROPERLY IDENTIFY THE PROBLEM

Often people use drugs to escape the truth. Even the bad habit of smoking cigarettes is used to escape reality for a short period of time. This is an emotional crutch. Some people don't want to face/accept the truth about themselves and why they haven't accomplished what they wanted to achieve by this point in their lives; doing well in school, graduating, getting a good job, providing for

their family, accomplishing career promotions, or reaching other goals and dreams. These people try to escape the truth and reality by using drugs to drift off on a high. But reality will be waiting for them when they come down off the high.

PROPERLY IDENTIFY THE PROBLEM

Why haven't you accomplished what you wanted to accomplish? Following the crowd? Is it poor time management? Did you need to spend more time studying in school? Do you need to spend more time with decision-making and problem-solving skills? Do you need to spend time in meditation and prayer? Do you have attitude problems? Are you defensive and angry? Are you carrying around jealously and resentment? Are your self- esteem and self- worth based on the wrong thing? Are you living beyond your means, trying to keep up with the Joneses?

PROPERLY IDENTIFY THE PROBLEM

Some people can't handle the grief, sorrow, anger, and confusion they experience when someone close to them dies. Don't try to escape your feelings through a temporary high. You have to deal with these feelings truthfully and realistically to get through the grieving process.

Some people can't understand, come to terms, or attain closure after being abused. They don't know what to do with the anger. They look for someone to blame. They seek revenge. They want to transfer the negative feelings and energy from themselves to someone else, usually back to the perpetrator of the abuse. Then often, the abuse victim becomes an abuser of others. If they can't offload the pain, anguish, and guilt, they usually try to escape through the use of drugs.

You can and should let the negative feelings go and rest assured that Karma will catch up to the predator. Forgive your abuser.

I am NOT SAYING STAY IN AN ABUSIVE SITUATION. DO NOT STAY WITH AN ABUSER.

Understand that abusers are human, and no human is perfect. Their abusive behavior developed from some negative source or cause. Ultimately it is an EGO problem; abusing or degrading others to make them feel better about themselves.

There is no need to feel guilt or shame because you were raped or abused. This is not a perfect world, and many sick people with the sick twisted need to dominate and overpower others to stroke their sick, unhealthy egos.

Let the negative energy go. Holding on to negativity will attract more negativity toward you. Find a reputable therapist. Join support groups. Set new short-term and long-term goals. Then reward yourself when you reach them. Find new creative hobbies; drawing, painting, WRITING, writing music, poetry, fiction, articles, or building model trains, planes and automobiles. But don't use drugs or another person as an emotional crutch.

There was a young lady named Roselyn Robeson. She and her sisters were repeatedly sexually abused by their father. She rushed into marrying a man to get away from her father and because she no longer wanted her father's last name. She didn't keep her husband sexually satisfied because she had understandable intimacy issues. This was not fair to him or to her. Yes, friends should help friends when they are in need. But this young lady needed professional psychological help, not necessarily a husband. They ended up divorcing for many reasons, mainly because he kept cheating on her.

PROPERLY IDENTIFY THE PROBLEM AND SELECT THE APPROPRIATE SOLUTION

CO-DEPENDENCY

A person's sanity is directly proportionate with their ability to comprehend and accept the truth. Some codependents have a distorted need to have someone dependent upon them. So, they enable the addict, facilitating continuous use so that the addict will keep leaning on them for help.

Some codependents feel guilty or somewhat responsible for the condition of the addict. Still, it is easier for them to keep the status quo instead of dealing with the situation in a mature, responsible manner.

PROPERLY IDENTIFY THE PROBLEM AND SELECT THE APPROPRIATE SOLUTION

Join support groups and seek professional help for all involved. But most importantly, understand who and what the ego is. Ego is not self-esteem or self-worth, or pride. If your self-esteem and self-worth are based on the right thing, not on ego, you will avoid many mental issues.

Self-esteem and self-worth should be based on doing the best you can with what you have been given. Self-esteem and self-worth should not be based on compare and compete.

CHAPTER TWELVE:

WHY BUY THE WHOLE PIG, WHEN ALL YOU REALLY WANT IS THE SAUSAGE

(Note: In this book, you will see many sentences, phrases, thoughts, and messages repeated several times. This is intentional. Because we are so indoctrinated and thoroughly saturated with the follower's way of thinking and the "old" way of doing things; new ideas, a new awareness and the process of transitioning philosophies, thoughts, and lifestyles, requires a repetitive presentation.)

MALE CHAUVINISM

The conqueror gets to write and re-write HIS-story to say whatever he chooses.

Many eons ago, after ego arrived on this planet, ego whispered into the ear of the human male and told him he should dominate the human species because of physical strength. This was the abominable sin. The divine feminine (the feminine connection to the divine) was severely suppressed, oppressed, stunted, abused and controlled. There were many ancient cities and nations ruled by women. The conqueror gets to write and re-write HIS - story to omit whatever he chooses. After ego possessed men, they reasoned they had the right to beat women into submission. Mature, competent, and enlightened (non-ego-driven) individuals know that just because you can do something, it does not mean you should do that thing. Women endured abuse and suppression because they had no other means to survive. If a woman tried to make it on

177

her own, she would be captured and dominated by another man or killed by wild animals.

The roles and full capabilities of women have been reemerging over the years. Still, in some parts of the world, it is legal for men to beat their wives. Still today, in some parts of the world, women are treated as second class citizens. Just as it was said during slavery about the slaves, that the slaves were inferior and incapable of learning to read and write. The same was said that women were intellectually inferior to men.

This has been proven to be untrue on both accounts. In modern times, we see that some women have achieved as much or even more academically, intellectually, and professionally as their male counterparts. Lookup: Sarah Breedlove, Dr. Mae Jemison and Ms. Stephanie Diana Wilson.

Who is Sarah Breedlove? Why don't we know "SARAH BREEDLOVE"!!?!!?

Who is Mr. Charles Joseph Walker?

I heard an African American man actually say, "It's the natural order of things." He was referring to men making the decisions and running the household. Slave owners used that same sentence and philosophy to justify slavery. They said it was the natural order of things.

They said Caucasians were superior intellectually, and therefore it was the natural law for whites to use, abuse, and controlblacks. Another African American man's web page said he wants a woman who knows her place in the boardroom and the bedroom.

What does he mean by "her place?" I wonder how this man would react to a Caucasian man if he said, "I like it when a nigger knows his place. Those people should be janitors. They don't belong in the boardroom unless they are cleaning it."

Does this African American man tell his daughter not to aspire to be a Chief Executive Officer or serve on the board of directors of a large corporation?

And what about your surname?

We know it is common practice for a woman to take the last name of her fiancé after the wedding ceremony, under the same philosophy as the slaves taking the last name of their masters. The owner bestows his name upon his property. Is a wife the property of her husband? Well, currently, we don't think of wives in that way. But during different periods in history, wives were undoubtedly considered to be the property of their husbands. And now, more often, we see the word obey taken out of the wedding vows.

I have recently studied and researched the teachings of many spiritual leaders who are considered enlightened and "woke" to the real truth. Often, I did my own verification of what teachings are, in fact, true and what is false. For me, the common point of disagreement is the correct and proper roles of women in the household and in their professional lives. Of course, I say; to each their own.

But answer me this: Who has the better decision-making skills? Who has the better problem-solving skills? Who is better organized? Who is better disciplined? Who has better money management skills? In some households, it is the woman, and in other households, it is the man. And still, in some places, it is a mixture of both. But you shouldn't think of it as a "W" or an "L" situation (a win or a loss). We are working for the best for the entire family. We are trying to make the BEST decisions possible for all involved.

I heard many male spiritual teachers get upset when discussing the term Toxic Masculinity. I guess the ego was too much in control of them and prevented them from taking the time to research and analyze the real definition of Toxic Masculinity. When the term is used, it is **not** referring to ALL masculinity.

The term is referring to only the portion of masculinity that is toxic. When masculinity is ego-driven, it has crossed the line into toxicity. This is toxic when a person uses physical strength, mental strength, psychological games, economic power, and executive power on offense for personal gain, pleasure, and unethical reasons. This is ego. If you are on a righteous defense and are protecting the life and safety of you and your family, then do what you gotta do. This is not toxic.

***THE BRAIN IN A FEMALE'S BODY IS EQUALLY CAPABLE AS THE BRAIN IN A

MALE'S BODY.***

THE KEY IS FOR WOMEN TO TRULY

BELIEVE THEY CAN ACHIEVE AS MUCH OR MORE THAN A MAN AND NOT BUY INTO THE FALSE PROPAGANDA THAT WOMEN ARE INTELLECTUALLY INFERIOR TO MEN.

Spiritually and metaphysically, many women have an advantage over many men. Have you heard of Women's Intuition, the Devine Feminine, or the Feminine Devine?

I am aware that both genders of the human Homosapien species have both masculine and feminine within them.

Some men like to perpetuate the false notion that women are intellectually inferior to men. The men who do this are men who have over inflated egos. They have a twisted need to degrade women in order to feel better about themselves. Some men hold on to the pre-historic definition of what it means to be a man. The commonly accepted definition of being a man has changed over the years.

Women used to be dependent on a man for food, shelter and clothing. Still, because some men have abused this dominance over women through mental abuse, physical abuse, neglect and infidelity, (absolute power corrupts, absolutely) out of necessity, a woman's role and the capabilities of women have slowly reemerged over the years.

Women can advance educationally and professionally. A woman does not have to tolerate abuse.

Why does she have to be SUB?

Why does she have to be SUB-ordinate for you to feel like a man?

Why does she have to be SUB -missive for your masculinity to be validated?

Why does she have to be less for you to feel adequate?

Why do you want to de-value {SUB - tract from} her intellect and capabilities?

Why do you have to put someone else down to make yourself feel better?

This is an indication that there is a bigger underlying problem within the man.

Do you teach your daughters only to strive to make the grade of "B" because "As" are only for boys? Do you tell your daughters to intentionally make mistakes on homework and when taking test, because "As" are for boys?

If she has developed her problem-solving skills" and decision-making skills," why shouldn't she use them to enhance her relationships?

Why does she have to "play the dumb role" to stroke your ego? ... and giggle at your corny jokes ...

You know... if you play the dumb role long enough, you will become dumb.

A real man of quality is not intimidated by a woman of equality.

When there is a disagreement, if you leave your ego out of it and honestly try to come up with the best solution, no matter who contributes the best solution, you are behaving in a mature, competent manner.

Why does it matter who comes up with the best solution? Leave your ego out of it. It is not about who gets their way. It is not about the "W" or the "L." It is not the person who gets their way - wins, and the other person is a loser.

Just be a mature, responsible adult and do what is best for the couple/family, no matter who comes up with the best solution.

Some men have a hard time accepting that SOME women are *IN FACT* more intelligent than they are. Why should she pretend to be less intelligent? Why should she hold back her talents? Why should she "PLAY" the dumb role? It is a team effort. She has your back, and she is very supportive of you. But she shouldn't lie to you just to stroke your ego. You need the honest, blatant truth, and you need it to come fromher.

... and vice versa

A man needs to have his woman's back. She needs to know she can count on him. He needs to be supportive of her. He should not lie to her just to stroke her ego. He needs to give her full honesty and blatant truth.

In a civilized society, there are rules and laws against physical abuse and assault. There are even laws regarding neglect, abandonment, and infidelity. Civilized humans can communicate and use reason and logic to resolve issues. This separates humans from other animals, who resort to physical violence on offence and defense, by instinct.

People often refer to the Bible passage that states that a woman should be submissive to her husband. Remember, the Bible was written back in history when most women were not allowed to advance educationally and professionally. This was also at a time in history when a man had the legal right to beat his wife into submission.

If a couple wants to abide by this religious belief, **before entering into matrimony**, they should make sure each individual is a STABLE, SECURE, and MATURE person. Make sure their partner is someone with whom they are compatible and have compatible short-term goals and, more importantly, compatible long-term goals. Marry someone who is not on an ego trip. A real man should not have to degrade or abuse a woman to stroke his ego. That is a sign of insecurity and immaturity. A man of real quality is not threatened by a woman of equality.

If there is a disagreement, the couple should use logic, reasoning and open communication to resolve the issue, not automatically let the man decide just because he is the male of the species. If a man is secure (confident) and mature, not on an ego trip, he will listen to logic and reasoning. If he brings Fact#1 and Fact # 2 to support his side of the discussion, and she brings Fact # 1, Fact # 2, Fact #3, and Fact # 4 to support her side. Which is the better choice? But don't confuse this with a W or an L. This is a logical, reasonable method of decision-making and problem-solving.

But so many people are on an ego trip, and they want to keep score as to who won the argument and who lost, so they can feel like they are "THE WINNER" of the argument. {don't confuse this with keeping track of who brought the most supporting facts to the table} It's not about stroking your ego. It's about finding the best solution, as mature; competent adults should do.

DEFINITIONS:

Conversation: an oral exchange of sentiments, observations, opinions, or ideas between two or more people.

Discussion: the action or process of talking about something to reach a decision or exchange ideas.

Debate: a formal discussion on a particular topic in a public meeting or legislative assembly, in which opposing opinions are put forward.

Argument: a reason or set of reasons given with the aim of persuading others that an action or idea is right or wrong.

Question: When does a discussion turn into an argument?

Answer: When EGO enters the room. When insults, zings and jabs enter the conversation [ego driven]. When you lose focus of the topic because of intentionally distracting defense mechanisms [bruised ego]. When it turns into a competition of who can cut the deepest, or who can list the most faults and mistakes of the other. [Compare & Compete]

Dear Sistaz: Don't let him play the "Angry Black Woman" card. Keep your ego out of it. BELIEVE ME! Just simply point out the facts of his errors (if his errors are the core topic of the discussion).

Don't worry ... THERE WILL BE PLENTY! Stay calm. There is no need for sarcasm, neck rolling, insults, or profanity. The facts will speak for themselves. He will try to play the "Angry Black Woman" card and distract you from the real issue – his mistakes.   Sincerely, Eileena

Not all black women are Angry.

Dear Sistaz, Don't get upset if someone calls you an angry black woman. It is a trap to trigger anger. If the shoe don't fit, then shut the fuck up. 😊 If you are not an angry black woman, then they are mistaken and in error when calling you an angry black woman. Just like it's a trap when they say, "You need to calm down." Well, that may or may not be a trap. You should stay calm. Don't get upset when someone says they are not attracted to you or don't want an angry black woman. Not all black women are angry black women. What sane person would like to be in a romantic relationship with an angry person? Ask yourself: "Am I an angry black woman?" ... If the shoe doesn't fit, then...   If the answer is yes, then get some self-help and therapy to dissipate the anger positively and constructively.   Best regards, Eileena

If a man wants his woman ignorant and dependent on him, he has insecurity and ego issues. If he thinks he controls his woman per the Bible, remember that it is a sin to waste God given talents and abilities. If a man is suppressing a woman's talents and capabilities, he is not following the Bible.

Someone asked the question, "Would you rather

be right and alone than wrong and keep your man?" Well, yes, I'd rather be alone until I find a man who will not ignore me and my intelligent contributions to the discussion.

I wouldn't want resentment to build from being ignored time and time again. That resentment could build up over time to become a dangerous eruption.

Some spiritual teachers say one of the major problems people have is always wanting to be right. The spiritual teachers ask, "Would you rather be right, or would you rather be happy?"

This question is error-ridden. The intent is in error. An alternate question could be: Would you rather win the argument, or would you rather be happy? But this is also an error- ridden question. The intent is in error.

PROPERLY IDENTIFY THE PROBLEM

The real problem is wanting to "WIN the ARGUMENT" at any cost and/or wanting to get the last word. Some ego driven people want to win the argument, whether they have logical supporting facts or not. Winning is definitely ego driven and an ego boost.

People want to WIN the argument. But "WINNING" is subject to interpretation. Winning is in the eye of the beholder. Some may say winning an argument is: who can shout the loudest. Some may see winning an argument as who can outlast or exhaust their opponent with complex double talk and persistency. Some see winning the argument as who can insult the hardest and cut the deepest with hurtful words and insults. Some see winning the argument as who can point out the most mistakes or the most egregious mistakes of the other person, which may or may not have anything to do with the current topic of discussion.

Regarding the question, "Do you want to be right, or do you want to be happy?" Of course, we all want to be correct, accurate, and logical. My definition of being right is presenting supporting facts and logical analysis of the details without emotion or ego. Being correct, accurate, and the most logical should automatically be the selected choice for resolution.

The spiritual teachers who asked "Would you rather win the argument, or would you rather be happy?" he sometimes recommends bowing out, giving in, or avoiding the confrontation, suggesting that this will make all parties involved; happier. I disagree with him. I recognize that resentment will build if individuals know they have the logical facts in their favor and they continuously bow out, give in, or avoid the confrontation.

This built-up resentment is a tangible, measurable ball of negative energy that will eventually manifest itself as an explosion of emotion, stress, or disease within the physical body. If this resentment has built up within a committed, romantic couple or any relationship, for example, professional relationship, familial relationship, friendships, BFF's, in these cases, disfunction and toxicity will grow, and a break-up will likely result.

The ego always keeps track of the Ws and the Ls, the

wins and losses. If you are a mature, competent adult with your ego under control, you will be willing and able to listen to the relevant facts, make a logical analysis, and reach a reasonable resolution.

I do whole-heartedly agree with: "Choosing your battles wisely." You should actually TAKE THE TIME to write down or cognitively weigh the pros and cons of different likely outcomes of going through with any confrontation.

If you bow out or give in, you must dissipate any resentment you may be harboring in a positive manner. If your ego is not involved and you are not keeping track of your wins and losses, you can easily let some confrontations go by merely saying, "It is not worth it."

Understand that some situations are not worth the negative emotion, the risk to the relationship, the cause and effect, or the consequences of the confrontation.

If you and your partner cannot come to calm, reasonable, logical resolutions, maybe you are not comparable.

Stop with the "We are two passionate people, and our arguments get heated, hot and heavy." That is nothin' but heated, hot, HEAVY, EGO.

USE IT OR LOSE IT!!!

If a woman does not learn, develop and MOST IMPORTANTLY USE decision-making" and problem-solving skills, she will lose these skills. Both men and women should take the time to highly develop their decision-making and problem-solving skills highly, so they can function independently and WITH CONFI DENCE. If your partner is away from you and is faced with a decision to make (at work, or with the children, or at an auto mechanic, or car dealership), you want her to be able to make good choices, on her own, with competence and confidence.

Over the years, men have neglected and abused women so severely that women had to develop themselves as the household's breadwinners. A family would be wise to have both parents capable of sustaining the home individually. I have seen so-called, "Church Ladies" resenting, gossiping and degrading women who have chosen to develop themselves educationally and professionally.

I have seen so much catty, petty jealously from these so-called "Church Ladies" who have let their men suppress them. Deep down inside, they resent their husbands for suppressing them and resent themselves for allowing themselves to be suppressed. Then, because they don't have the means to support themselves, they feel trapped, which leads to more hateful jealous behavior.

There is an abundance of comparing and competing and "Keeping Up with the Joneses" in the Church. On the other hand, can an educated, professional woman date a blue-collar, working-class male? Will they have mature, intellectually stimulating conversations? Is he active in pursuing educational and career advancement? Will his ego get in the way? Will her ego get in the way? Is their preference for entertainment compatible? Will he feel comfortable at her professional functions and events? Are their short-term and long-term goals compatible? Will he be able to withstand taunting and sarcastic remarks from outsiders regarding the relationship?

If a man is confident, mature and intelligent, he will appreciate mature and intelligent decision-making contributions from his woman.

But the male chauvinist doesn't really think of his woman as a peer, or equal, or a mature competent adult. They think of women as objects, acquisitions and possessions. Men are less willing to forgive infidelity because their ego will be brutally damaged if another man can brag that he had the other man's woman.

Of course, he feels the pain from betrayal and loss of trust. Because the chauvinistic male's ego is based (in part) on other people's opinion, if another man can brag, laugh and have others laugh at the chauvinist, his ego will be severely damaged.

The chauvinist doesn't want the other guy feeling he has something on the chauvinist, or have the other guy feeling superior or looking down on him. Also, he can't stand to be compared to another guy.

He wants to think he has overwhelmed his woman like he blew her mind (outsmarted her). He actually wants to control her, and take away her free will. I heard some men say it is worse when a woman cheats because "He was inside of her" as if she was magically and mystically, overwhelmingly, filled with his soul, spirit and essence. This is a clear demonstration that he doesn't think of her as equally intelligent, mature and competent.

We all know that sexual encounters range from "just a fuck" to an intense expression of emotion, passion and love through making love.

Women categorize sexual encounters the same as men do. Making love can be just as intense and spiritual for a man as for a woman.

What is the significance of "He was inside of her"?

Is it the act of penetration? Is it the submissive act of allowing penetration?

"A friend," told me that during some hot, steamy, intense sex, she shoved her fingers into her man's mouth, and he sucked them. So, therefore, she was inside of him. RIGHT!?!

What's with the exaggerated drama? He wants to think he has overwhelmed his woman like she's some zombie –robot (Stepford Wife) repeating, "In will only fuck Mike. I will only fuck Mike". This would stroke his ego.

Yes, there are some spiritual, physical and metaphysical effects of sexing and exchanging/absorbing bodily fluids for both men and women. But you can use spiritual and physical barriers to prevent unwanted exchanges, attachments, and residual effects. You can cleanse your body before and after the act and cleanse/clear your aura before and after the act.

The male chauvinist ego wants to believe he is superior to females. Because his self- esteem is based on compare and compete, he looks for any opportunity to degrade another person to make himself feel better. He looks for any opportunity to belittle women to make himself feel bigger.

The biggest cause for tension, disagreement and break-up of a romantic couple is competition between the two people within the couple. They want to be able to manipulate and control the other person. They want the most "W's" and the least "L's" from the disagreements. They want to be the breadwinners, thinking this should give them control of how the money is spent. They get jealous if their partner has a more illustrious, respectable, powerful job/career.

STOP COMPARING AND COMPETING WITH YOUR SPOUSE/PARTNER!

Women, who choose to let a man suppress them should ask why they allow this? Being a follower is no excuse or justification. You were just "FOLLOWING" tradition. [NO EXCUSE] You were just doing what you were told. [NO EXCUSE] Who told Harriett Tubman she could create and operate the Underground Railroad? Was she following tradition? Was she letting a man make her decision? Nobody, No, and Hell No.

Use your God-given skills and abilities. It is a sin not to live up to your full potential. Remember, most people only use 10 % of their brain's capability during their lifetime. THE SKY IS THELIMIT! If a man suppresses a woman, he has ego issues, and a woman should not ENTER into a relationship with a man with these ego problems. To the MEN: If a woman truly loves and respects you for the REAL you (not some macho FAKE front you are displaying), you don't have to worry about her leaving you or disrespecting you.

Work on self-improvement and make yourself someone worthy of her love, devotion, loyalty, trust and respect. Men also have a greater fear that the woman will compare him to other men. That's also why they worry about how many partners the woman has had. He doesn't want to lose in the comparison, and he doesn't want the other man to brag that he had the woman. If you both come to the relationship with a clean bill of health, don't worry about past partners. If you don't have a clean bill of health, you must be honest with your potential partner about your condition. You only really need to discuss how to mitigate contagion and establish clearly identifiable expressed consent. The number of past partners is not a necessary divulgence.

Question: Why do men cheat?

Answer: EGO. Actually, it's testosterone, but they are almost inseparable {Ego and Testosterone}.

It's EGO; in that, they want to feel that they have gotten away with something, they've gotten over on somebody, they've outsmarted somebody, they've manipulated somebody, and they've conquered somebody, payback or revenge.

1. Got away with something: he didn't get caught. He made up a plan, a story, an alibi.

2. Got over on somebody: He told a lie, and she believed him.

3. Outsmarted/Manipulated/Conquered someone: She was a "good girl." She didn't want to do it. She was seduced. He "out-macked" another person for her attention.

4. Payback/Revenge: He lost an argument. She emasculated him. He couldn't control her. She got her way against his wishes. He suspects she cheated on him.

All of these things will give them an "EGO BONUS POINT."

Also, fear of commitment, self-sabotage, and immaturity are underlying or contributing reasons why men cheat—still ego.

Why do men get caught more often than women? Answer: Arrogance and EGO. They underestimate the intelligence of their significant other.

All infidelity is 100% caused by ego. Whether a male or a female does it, all cheating is 100% caused by ego.

Women cheat for the same cause and effect of the items previously mentioned. People want to sound all deep and philosophical by saying women cheat for emotional reasons or emotional support. But after you pick it apart, analyze it and boil it down, it really is ego.

Go back and read items #1 thru #4 listed previously and switch the gender roles. Picture a woman doing these things instead of a man. If a woman has her self-esteem and self- worth based on the right thing, she will be secure and confident about herself as an individual. If she doesn't need to have "a man " to validate or justify her existence, she won't hesitate to exit a toxic, dysfunctional, lop-sided relationship.   She won't need to cheat, in secret, to put a Band-Aid on the real problem or camouflage the real problem.

PROPERLY IDENTIFY THE PROBLEM

You must understand that ego, self- esteem, and pride have very different meanings. If a man or a woman is letting someone other than their spouse/partner stroke their ego by giving them attention or flattering and complimenting them, this is ego-driven. If your self-esteem is based on the right thing, you won't be swayed or influenced by superficial, external things like attention, flattery or compliments. Self- esteem and self-worth are internal projects, not external projects. If you don't understand this by now, go back and read Chapter One.

I had heard some people say the affair helped keep their marriage together because they were able to escape the reality of their tragic, toxic marriage for a little while and get me stress relief before they had to go back home.

Why not just end the dysfunctional, toxic relationship? Is it cheaper to keep her? Is it worth always having that ticking timebomb of the truth hanging around in the background? Is it worth the risk? Because when a ticking time bomb finally explodes, there is a great deal of unpredictable, uncalculated collateral damage. Is it worth the risk?

Some people say that men can have sex with another human being, and it does not mean anything. Sex between humans 100% of the time has 100% significant meaning: consciously, subconsciously, physically, metaphysically, spiritually, medically, morally and ethically.

You need to know the causes and effects of coitus on and from every aspect, angle, astral plane and dimension listed in the previous sentence. If it didn't mean anything, you would just go somewhere and jack off. Why do you need to interact with another human?

Stop saying it doesn't mean anything. That is a total lie. The energy you release will come back to you, negative or positive.

Now, let's go back to the testosterone. When you look at little boys playing and look at little girls playing, even as toddlers, you can see the difference. Even before the nurturing and societal norms are taught, you can see the difference. Little boys are more physically aggressive and rough-edged. This is caused by males having more testosterone than females. Then add the nurturing, societal norms, and double standards, and the result is the male macho ego.

Why do athletes use testosterone or derivatives thereof to enhance performance? Why is this illegal? What are the side effects? In addition to increasing muscle mass, it also induces aggressive, egotistical behavior. You may have heard of "Roid Rage", where steroids user spin in and out of control, anger and rage.

"To whom much is given, much is required."

"To whom more testosterone is given (by God, not by your trainer or coach), much more maturity and discipline is required."

As opposed to the cavemen days, civilized society has laws against physical abuse, laws forbidding assault and battery. Mature, civilized men use intellect, reasoning and diplomacy to resolve disagreements.

Mature, civilized men, who have their self-esteem based on the right thing and not even partially based on the opinions of others, will not lose their temper over immature name- calling or taunting. He can even withstand physical abuse. He should remove himself from a physically abusive situation. He should only use physical strength on defense, not offense, if the situation is life-threatening.

A mature, secure, intelligent, self- confident man does not need to seek and try to earn "EGO BONUS POINTS" whenever and wherever possible. Some immature, insecure people look for (actually seek out) situations to degrade, embarrass, and demean others to gain "EGO

BONUS POINTS" and pick, prod and instigate to start fights.

I heard a man say that he thinks some men cheat because men are not monogamists by nature. I'm afraid I have to disagree; I think men are on a bigger ego trip – "BY NATURE". It's testosterone. It is also the degree to which they are mature and secure.

A mature, secure man doesn't need to feel that he has gotten away with something, he has gotten over on somebody, he has outsmarted somebody, he has manipulated somebody, he has conquered somebody, payback or revenge.

Some say men are not monogamists by nature because the male body produces thousands of sperm per month as opposed to the female body only producing one egg per month.

God (your higher power, your creator) has given you the blessing of free will, and the FREEDOM of choice. Don't be a slave to your instincts. You are of the species Homosapien. Use your powers for good. God chose humans over all the creatures of the earth to bless with the gift of advanced intelligence. "To whom much is given, much is required."

And a mature, secure man who has a quality compatible partner/wife at home won't want to jeopardize that relationship with infidelity. If something is lacking, missing, or disagreeable at home, the mature, intelligent, secure person can effectively communicate and resolve the issue, keeping the ego under control.

In some situations, a person who doesn't want to commit to a relationship and regularly wants to have multiple sex partners is "copping out". They might not have the skills or patience for problem-solving. If a disagreement arises, or the situation feels too intense, they want to duck out and skip over to their other lover. That way, they can avoid and maybe never resolve the real issue.

A strong family structure is essential for children. Look at the statistics on a single parent or unplanned births among the races in the 1960s, the 1980s, and the 2000s.

https://www.census.gov/data/tables/time-series/demo/families/families.html

A race of accidents! What are the implications? What kind of future will there be? Where is the man's responsibility in that, as the assumed leaders of the community and head of household?

The man who said that men are not monogamists by nature also said these men should be completely honest with all of their lovers about their other lovers. I do agree with that statement.

But I hope the women who knowingly sleep with/have a relationship with a non-monogamist man (don't forget about STI's), I hope they are completely honest with themselves and ask themselves why they are accepting this type of relationship? If you can honestly say, you don't feel any pain, jealously, degradation, or guilt when you know he is with someone else, HONESTLY!? Then OK. But if you have any of those feelings, they will eat away at you and eventually, it will eat you up. You will lose your self-respect completely, or there will be a confrontation, or you will get out of it, then you will ask yourself why you wasted your time in this dysfunctional, toxic relationship.

Why wouldn't you want a man to love, honor, respect, cherish, and truly adore you and give you the kind of commitment you want and deserve?

Would this man tell his daughter to settle for a relationship with a man who sleeps around because this is the best she can hope for? Would he tell his daughter that twisted lie that men are not monogamist by nature?

And why would a man want to spread himself that thin, between two or three girlfriends or two or three baby mommas and babies? No matter how much money you have in the bank, you cannot buy more time. There are twenty-four hours in a day. All the money in the world will not buy you twenty-five, twenty-six or twenty-seven hours in a   day.

Can you spend REAL * QUALITY * time with all of your girlfriends and all of your children? Special   occasions?   Holidays?   Birthdays? Vacations? What if there is a medical or another type of emergency in two different households simultaneously?

There is a definite correlation between ego and sex-drive. For some people, the act of having sex translates into filling a void for lack of attention and affection or lack of self-esteem, and sex is fulfilling the erroneous requirement to earn "EGO BONUS POINTS."

With cheaters and players, it is not just the physical. It is not just a high sex drive that makes them sleep around. If it were simply a physical need, then they would just resort to masturbation or other artificial devices. But the ego is apparent because of the need to interact with another human being.

The ego boost comes from the acknowledgment from another human being and the superficial validation that another human being is willing to give you attention and pleasure. The ego boost and psychological satisfaction come from the feeling that you have gotten away with something, you've gotten over on somebody, you've outsmarted somebody, you've manipulated somebody, you've conquered somebody, payback or revenge, or because you lost an argument with your wife/girlfriend.

When the *QUALITY* becomes more important than the quantity, you know you are on the right path. And that quality comes with someone who knows you very well (and vice versa), and you can connect in a higher spiritual dimension, transcending the physical. An orgasm formulates and occurs more between the ears than between the legs.

Have you read the Kama Sutra? Have you explored Tantra? Venus Butterfly?

Once you reach that level with your partner, you will have very little to no desire to waste your time with basic sex and a basic partner. And you will patiently wait for that quality during extended absences and business trips. Remember, most people only use 10% of their brain capability during their lifetime.

What about your sexual capability and capacity? HHHHHHhhhhhhhhmmmmmmmmmmmm?

Let's take this to the next level! To the tenth power! Exponentially!

"Followers," you are not even scratching the surface!

****

There is such a thing as spiritual ego. Learning, gaining understanding, increasing intelligence, and ascending to the net level of consciousness and enlightenment is stimulating and exhilarating. But when ego is involved, and hence the compare and compete, ego is boosted because it recognizes its host is more knowledge than the average person. The egotistical pride comes from the statement, "I'm smarter than you." When you are on the path, actively and intentionally seeking enlightenment, that information will start to present itself to you at an ever-increasing pace.

"When the student is ready, the teacher will appear."   -Tao Te Ching

You soon realize, I've started down this rabbit hole, and it is never ending. Yes, knowledge is infinite. The rabbit hole is infinite. Your next realization or question is; why did it take so long for me to come across this information? Who else knows? How long have they known? Maybe only a select few in the secret society have known or maybe a vast number a certain race or religious sector have this knowledge. While there are a great number that do know, there is still an even greater number that don't know.

That's when spiritual ego becomes a problem; feeling you are superior because you have this set of knowledge that so many others do not have.

STAY HUMBLE! Because knowledge is infinite. The rabbit hole is infinite. We ALL are only scratching the surface. It is likely you will encounter someone who is miles ahead if you down the rabbit hole and will put you and your ego to shame with the vast knowledge they have acquired.

Many spiritual leaders soon run into the problem of spiritual ego. Spiritual leaders are revered, respected, loved and praised. The kind of spiritual leader who wants, needs and receives an ego boost from having followers is the kind of spiritual leader who develops spiritual ego problems. Followers by definition and nature want and need to be told what to do and think.
Most followers do not do very much of their own research, they just want to be mindlessly led around. The ego driven spiritual leader will capitalize on this opportunity to manipulate, mold, groom, and scam their vulnerable, naive followers, knowing they are hungry and thirsty to be lead.

STAY HUMBLE! Don't let it go to your head. Recognize who and what ego truly is.

In the documentary: "The Vow," S1, E8, there is a scene

where Anthony Ames is talking to Mark Vicente, [between 39 min and 41 min]. Mr. Ames says: "Can I re-frame it for you? The arrogance, pride and the sanctimonious nature at which we went about what we thought we were building, our pride is the thing that helped facilitate it."

Mr. Ames was a follower within this organization. Their egos had gotten too big. This is most likely because their leader's ego had grown way too big and way out of control. Most of the people within this organization had/have over inflated egos. That is why so many of them are having such a hard time reconciling their affiliation and actions within the organization with current reality.

PART 4:

RELEASE THE CATS!

CHAPTER THIRTEEN:

HOW MUCH IS THATWOMAN IN THE WINDOW? HOW DO I VALUE MY SELF-IMAGE?

(Note: In this book, you will see many sentences, phrases, thoughts, and messages repeated several times. This is intentional. Because we are so thoroughly indoctrinated and thoroughly saturated with the follower's way of thinking and the "old" way of doing things; new ideas, a new awareness and the process of transitioning philosophies, thoughts, and lifestyles; requires a repetitive presentation.)

Women are constantly comparing themselves to each other to get their "EGO BONUS POINTS." The "FOLLOWER" woman follows the popular definition of beauty. All people (men and women) should strive to be HEALTHY and PHYSICALLY FIT and "DO THE BEST YOU CAN WITH WHAT YOU'VE BEEN GIVEN."

Not every woman is supposed to have clothing sizes in the single digits. It varies according to your DNA, which determines your family traits, bone structure, muscle density, etc.

All people should strive to be healthy and physically fit. Don't worry about what other people think and what others are doing because your self-worth and self-image should have nothing to do with other people's opinions. Don't be a "FOLLOWER" and have to compare your body with everyone you see, trying to get your

"EGO BONUS POINTS." Don't let outside pressures (the media, friends, family) push you to be unhealthy or unrealistic.

PROPERLY IDENTIFY THE PROBLEM

If someone develops an eating disorder trying to look more like a model in a fashion magazine, the basis of their self-esteem and self-worth is the problem. The magazine is not the problem. Stop compare ad compete with the models in the magazine. Stop following the crowd's definition of beauty. Do the best you can with what you've been given.

(Please recognize there is a difference between being overweight and OBESITY)

There are **obese** people and obese enablers who say, "love yourself", and "accept yourself", and "Be Big & Beautiful." These people are in denial and lying to themselves. All people should strive to be healthy and physically fit. Obesity is unhealthy. Obesity leads to a whole slew of health and emotional problems.

It's not fun taking medication and monitoring diabetes, injecting insulin and monitoring high blood pressure, circulation problems, skin rashes, and chaffing. It's not fun having limbs amputated, going blind, and even dying. Shopping for clothing can be frustrating as well.

Obese people lie to themselves and try to overlook their problems on a conscious level, but they are still frustrated, angry, and jealous on other subconscious levels. They still do petty superficial, sometimes mean and vengeful things to vent their frustrations and "EARN EGO BONUS POINTS."

A person's sanity is directly proportionate to their ability to comprehend and accept "THE TRUTH." Stop lying to yourself about being obese. Stop encouraging others to stay obese with you. "Misery loves company." Stop lying to yourself about being overweight. You are still frustrated, angry and jealous of smaller people. You are still doing petty superficial, sometimes mean and vengeful things to vent your frustrations and "EARN your EGO BONUS POINTS." Some people are still trying to push that "Beauty is on the in- side" and a man (or woman) shouldn't discriminate against you because you are fat. Being obese is (in many cases) an indicator of a possible lack of self- control, a possible lack of discipline, and may be an indicator that the person may carry anger, insecurity, and jealousy.

Why would anyone want to be with a person whose lack of self-control and lack of discipline has caused them to eat themselves into a state of being where their life is in danger?

I understand that other medical issues may cause obesity, and because of those medical conditions, a person's weight may be very tough to control. I'm not talking to you, right now.

We say people who are suicidal have a sick mentality because they are self- destructive. If you have allowed your weight to get to a level where your life - or quality of life is in danger {either your weight is too high or too low}, you are self-destructive, and this is a big problem. The first step in problem-solving is to properly identify the problem. Why are you obese?

... Overeating? ...Eating the wrong (unhealthy) food? ...Eating at the wrong time of day? ...Lack of exercise? ...Emotional eating? ... Hanging on to being fat as a defense mechanism (keeping others at a distance)? ... Other psychological issues? Properly identify the problem.

The formula has not changed: Burn more calories than you eat, and you will lose weight.

The medical textbooks definition of healthy is being free from infirmity; all vital signs and indicators are at healthy levels, such as weight, blood pressure, blood sugar level, heart rate, vital organs functioning properly, absence of life-threatening, debilitating diseases.

The components of physical fitness are muscular strength, muscular endurance, flexibility, body composition (body fat percent), cardiorespiratory endurance.

Just because a person is small doesn't mean they are healthy and/or physically fit. Being small just might be their natural state because of inherited traits. Some women want to be small, no matter the cost.

Some develop eating disorders. Some think it makes them superior to be smaller. Some experience the VERY UNHEALTHY Yo-Yo effect from fad dieting. And some undergo risky cosmetic surgical procedures.

This is why you shouldn't compare and compete to get your "EGO BONUS POINTS" or to contribute to the determination of your self- worth and self-esteem. You don't know all of the components that go into making a person look the way they do. It will NEVER be a valid or equal comparison. Two people can be on the same diet and exercise regimen and still have very different results. Do not compare and compete to determine your self-worth.

"DO THE BEST YOU CAN WITH WHAT YOU'VE BEEN GIVEN."

Look at your body and say, "This is what my creator has givento me." If you eat right and exercise regularly, consult a medical doctor, a certified nutritionist, and a certified personal trainer for recommendations; AND FOLLOW THEIR ADVICE; you will be doing the best you can with what you have been given.

Body fat percent is a better indicator of health than your scale weight or your dress size. Learn the difference between the literal definition of FAT and the slang meaning of PHAT.

Learn the difference between the literal definition of healthy and the slang meaning of healthy.

Stop crying about people teasing you, fat-shaming you, saying mean things to you and joking about you because you are fat. Your self-esteem shouldn't be based on their opinion anyway. Your self-esteem should be based on doing the best with what you've been given. So, are you doing the best you can with what you've been given? If not, make a plan.

Start your step-by-step journey to getting there.

It is an internal, personal, private issue. You don't have to explain or justify your condition to anyone. But you do need to be completely honest with yourself in your personal, private, quiet introspection time. So, ask yourself, who is at fault for you being fat? Is it you and your lack of self- control? If your significant other encourages you and enables you to be Fat/Phat - unhealthy, your significant other has some sick, distorted psychological issues. Someone with a healthy mental status would not want their partner to be unhealthy. That should be obvious.

Remember the serenity prayer: Lord help me to change the things I can change, accept the things I cannot change, and grant me the wisdom to know the difference.

Set SMART, realistic healthy physical fitness goals.

S: specific, sustainable, strengthening
M: measurable, meaningful, motivational
A: attainable, achievable, action-oriented
R: realistic, relevant, rewarding
T: Time based goals. Set milestones, target dates, and dead lines.

I have heard people say: "I just want to be fit."

Do you mean physically fit? Well ... what does that mean? If you are setting smart fitness goals, you must be very specific when defining your goals.

Do you know what your target heart rate is?

Set your SMART physical fitness goal and find out what target heart rate will best facilitate that goal. There is a different target heart rate for (1) healthy heart, (2) increasing endurance, (3) burning fat, (4) increasing speed.

Did you know if you take your heart rate too high, it can be counterproductive? You will start burning muscle mass as fuel instead of fat or sugar/carbs. You never want to burn muscle mass as fuel. Don't compete against the person on the treadmill next to you. They may have different fitness goals and may be working at a level not conducive to your fitness goals.

A healthy body helps create and maintain a healthy mind, and a healthy mind helps create and maintain a healthy body. Regular exercise creates more receptors in the brain, relieves stress, releases endorphins, rejuvenates the digestive system/immune system, among many other benefits.

You are not realistic if you are trying to have a smaller waist, to have an hourglass shape, when your creator gave you a box- shaped body. It's ok to want "SIX PACK" abs; check your motives. Are you trying to compare and compete with someone? Are you intentionally trying to make someone jealous? Are you trying to earn "EGO BONUS POINTS?"

Are you going to be frustrated and mad if you cannot attain this goal? Do you get jealous and upset when you see someone else with a smaller and more shapely body? Do you get mad and jealous when your mate is looking/lusting at another person?

People tell you to love yourself, but they don't tell you how.

Did you know that real trust has to be earned over time? Some people may be willing to take a calculated risk on you on the spot, but real trust is earned over time. Did you know that respect has to be earned over time? New acquaintances may show you common courtesy and use good manners, but real respect is earned over time. Real Love is earned over time. Someone may instantaneously treat you with humanity and dignity and show you common courtesy, but real love is earned over time. Likewise, **real** self-love is earned over time.

You know consciously and subconsciously whether you are worthy of love or not. You know all of your own deep, dark, dirty little secrets, all the lies, misleadings, manipulations and failures. Some people try to negotiate and mitigate by saying their good deeds outweigh their bad deeds. But your subconscious is smarter than that.

When you have earned your own love and self-respect, you can say, "I set my goals to ultimately do good, directly or indirectly, and to contribute good things to this world. I am continuously reaching my short-term and long- term goals. When I face obstacles, I find a way to overcome them. Some obstacles take longer to overcome than others, and some obstacles cause me to re-evaluate whether the goal is still worth pursuing or not. I have done my self-help, introspection analysis, and character building. I have done the work to become a mature, competent adult, overcoming juvenile petty jealousies and insecurities. I am not vengeful or cruel. I love and take care of my family and friends to the best of my abilities."

So, do the work and make yourself lovable.

Yes, you must learn to forgive yourself when you make a mistake. But consider this, how many times will you forgive a friend or family member for repeating the same mistake, over and over again. Yes, you should forgive as many times as the offense occurs, but with friends and family, at some point, you may have to start distancing and disassociating to protect your peace.

How do you do that with yourself? How do you keep forgiving yourself if you keep repeating the same mistakes over and overagain?

You must make a plan. Identify the triggers that compel you to repeat the same mistakes. Plan and role play/practice the words and actions to prevent repeating the same mistake. Work on your problem-solving skills. Work on your decision-making skills.

Do the work and make yourself lovable.

CHAPTER 14: Most Cats Have Green Eyes. Jealousy Does Not Become You

(Note: In this book, you will see many sentences, phrases, thoughts and messages repeated several times. This is intentional. Because we are so thoroughly indoctrinated, saturated and inundated with the follower's way of thinking and the "old" way of doing things; ... new ideas, a new awareness, and the process of transitioning philosophies, thoughts, and lifestyle requires repetitive presentation.)

Some heterosexual women have self- esteem issues with having or not having a man. The "FOLLOWER" women feel that it is a badge of accomplishment to "have a man." Yes, pro-creation is necessary and committed intimate relationships can be rewarding and fulfilling, but individuals need to be emotionally whole and stable BEFORE entering the relationship.

You have to come to a relationship with stability, or this will cause additional problems. If your self-worth and self- esteem are based on the wrong thing - something unstable like comparing yourself to others, then you are destined for additional frustrations and problems

Jealousy, insecurity, power struggles, neglect, and abuse all come from self-esteem/self-worth issues.

JEALOUSY; please don't get mad if your man looks/lusts/talks to another woman. They are going to look just like you are going to look, and it's not disrespectful to look. It is disrespectful to give a prolonged look, or a flirtatious look, or to "catcall," make suggestive sounds, or bite your lip or finger. It is disrespectful to ask for someone's phone number and/or ask for a date in front of or even behind your mates back. Neither you nor your mate should ever intentionally try to make the other jealous. That would be IMMATURE, IGNORANT, and DISRESPECTFUL.

This will lead to other problems in the relationship. If your mate treats you in an IMMATURE, IGNORANT and DISRESPECTFUL manner, you should both seek counseling to correct this behavior, but if this doesn't help, you should end the relationship.

JEALOUSY comes from not being realistic and not accepting who you really are. Constantly comparing and competing with others trying to "EARN EGO BONUS POINTS" leads to frustrations, envy, and negativity.

If you are mature, secure, and realistic about yourself, you won't feel threatened by your mate looking/lusting and talking to another person. If your mate is intentionally trying to make you jealous, you should consider leaving the relationship. That is a sure sign of egotistical behavior, intended to cause hurt and pain.

Here is a bit of bitter, nasty, naked truth, advice: you SHOULD have a positive outlook, give 100%, and expect the best for the relationship, but always have a contingency plan. The REALITY is that you can't control the thoughts and actions of another person. If a person really wants to leave you, they WILL leave you.

People can manipulate and influence others. But ultimately, it is that individual's decision to stay or go.

Some women have allowed themselves and their children to be abused because they want to keep up the appearance of a happy home. Part of their self-esteem is based on the opinions of others.

It's so unfortunate that some women tolerate abuse because they don't have the economic means to support themselves and their children. Part of their self-esteem is based on being able to say, "I have a man." Please teach your daughters (and sons) to be independent. Never sell your soul to "Have a man." Always have a backup plan and funds stashed away for a rainy day.

Don't be Jelly! 😊

Yes, you can admire and respect the accomplishments and acquisitions of others. Just understand their higher power determined it appropriate for them to have the possessions that they have.

It has been God's will to grant or withhold specific blessings, and that's why they have what they have, and it is God's will to grant or withhold specific blessings for you. Certain circumstances are beyond your control. Live within your means. Stop trying to "Keep Up with The Joneses." Check your motives. Don't base your self-esteem on material possessions. CHECK YOUR MOTIVES.

There is nothing wrong with having nice things. CHECK YOUR MOTIVES. Why do you want these things? Is it because you want to "OUT DO" someone else? Are you competing? Are you trying to keep up? Are you trying to impress? Are you trying to make someone jealous? CHECK YOUR MOTIVES.

Some people buy luxury cars because they appreciate fine craftsmanship, safety rating, and a reliable, highly reputable automobile company. They appreciate the artistic uniqueness, it is a smart, shrewd investment, and they can afford it.

CHECK YOUR MOTIVES.

If you are intentionally making someone jealous, and what goes around comes around, then they or someone else will intentionally make you jealous. This vicious cycle will continue to spiral and escalate into dysfunctional, toxic behavior and relationships. Also, pushing people to live beyond their means, puts their families and credit at risk.

Ask yourself, "Do you need to work harder and make better decisions and choices to afford to get the things you want and need? For the right reasons?"

For those who believe in reincarnation: Your creator has equipped you with everything you need to journey through this lifetime. Meditate and listen to your spirit guides. If you keep ignoring them, they will get quieter and quieter each time.

Out purchasing and outclassing your

siblings/family, co-workers and classmates is never your **assignments** during any incarnation.

For what shall it profit a man if he gains the whole world and lose his own **soul**?   Mark 8:36

Obtaining virtues (patience, kindness, being helpful and charitable) and building a noble character, learning to forgive, learning unconditional love, and taking the high road, is always part of your **assignment**. If you fail, your **soul** cannot ascend to the next level. You have to keep coming back, lifetime after lifetime, to try get a pass the grade.

Many people resort to illegal means to get money to purchase high priced material possessions because their self-esteem is based (in part) on material possessions. They are "Followers." They follow the popular belief that having certain, specific material possessions makes them better than others. They compare and compete to stroke their egos. They are comparing their material possessions to others, and if they feel they come out with the better item, they gain an "EGO BONUS POINT." If they don't have the better item in the comparison, then they lose an "EGO BONUS POINT."

\Other people scheme, lie, cheat, connive, step on other people get to ahead to obtain material possessions because their self-worth is based on material possessions. So before you respect, admire, or (if you're shallow) become jealous of another person's material possessions, remember you don't know the true source of these possessions unless this person is a close family member or close friend.

I met this guy, who had recently been released from prison. He was bragging about how he bought his first house at the ageof nineteen. He sold drugs and used that money to buy the house and many other material possessions. At the point in time at which I met him, he had nothing. Because of his imprisonment, he had lost everything.

There is a higher risk of attaining material possessions in the wrong way (illegally, cheating, lying, stepping on others). Ignorant, immature individuals can't see the big picture. Or they may accept the risk, going for instant gratification, popularity and acceptance.

Some people who resort to illegal practices to earn a living say they do it because they have no other way to make a living or feed their children. But the United States is truly the land of opportunity. How much money is enough? Or are you trying to out bling everybody?

Some women say they find it hard to maintain friendships with other females. (I can relate) If you are not a follower, and you are not a "yes" person, if you are not a gossiper, if you are not afraid to express your opinion even if it is not the popular, trending opinion, if you don't need to have everyone like you, if you don't fit into the social, group, clique construct where you may or may not be the alpha, then you may experience difficulty maintaining friendships with female groups. You may find one good BFF. But if your one good BFF has other female friends in other cliques, she may get pulled in two different directions.

Side Bar: some people like to use the "Common Denominator" analogy or metaphor. But most of these people don't really understand the division and multiplication of fractions, which is from where the term comes. There is more than one type of denominator. More to the point, there can be many common denominators. Where these dubiously philosophical and analytical amateurs go wrong is that they don't understand the significant difference between the terms "least common denominator" and "common denominator." Other common de- nominators are common belief systems, traditions, common courtesy, groupthink, the **follower mentality,** trying to follow the crowd, trying fit into the crowd, trying to fit into the popular clique, corporate culture, group and social dynamics, **pervasive ignorance**, people on the left side of the IQ bell curve, hierarchies, and bureaucracies.

When doing self-help, character building, and introspection, you should consider all contributing factors, variables, and denominators. Do not take fault for something that is not your fault. But do own your own mistakes. Some women have difficulty with female friendships because they are constantly comparing and competing, trying to one-up their friends. Some women have difficulty with female friendships because they are ego- driven, arrogant and self-centered. Some women who have difficulty with female friendships often say snide remarks, negative remarks, sarcasm, zingers, and jabs. Sarcasm is defined as the use of irony to mock or convey contempt.

Sarcasm does not demonstrate that you are clever, intelligent, or witty. I heard someone define sarcasm as anger disguised with humor. The intent is negative. There is a significant difference between laughing with someone and laughing at someone. Then they want to say: "Oh, you can't take a joke." But they are not really joking. Their intention is negative, and their intention is to cause hurt.

I do like comedy. I like comedy movies, and I like going to comedy clubs and shows. I don't like comedians who use the stage to vent their anger and disguise it as jokes. A female comedian at a comedy club in Los Angeles spent her whole set dogging out men.

While I agreed with most of the things she said, that was not my idea of comedy. As I said previously, I do like comedy, and I can take a joke. I recognize when the intent is for humor and laughter and when the intent is to be meant, to cause hurt, pain, and embarrassment.

I can take a joke, but I intentionally can't take a hint. I appreciate when a person has the courage to say what they mean and mean what they say. Don't hide behind sarcasm. Let's talk it over, like mature, intelligent, competent adults and see if your opinions or complaints are valid. But some people don't really, really want to clear the air. Their egos are dysfunctionally and toxically thriving on drama and negativity.

Try to ignore snide remarks, sarcasm, zings and jabs. The ignorant, immature people say these things to get a specific negative reaction from you, and sometimes they will keep pushing until they get that specific reaction.

That's when you know you need to minimize your interaction with that person as much as possible. It is not that you are thin- skinned or can't take a joke, but why would you want to be around someone who intentionally sends negativity your way? Why would you want to socialize with ignorant, immature people?

I like nice clothes, not necessarily expensive clothes, not necessarily designer clothes. I like to get quality products. I like to get my money's worth. I am sometimes willing to accept the trade-off when quality is lacking. "You get what you pay for." I grew up in a house with two parents who got up each and every weekday morning, bathed, dressed in business professional attire and went to work. They were great role models for me.

Some people naturally have style and class. Some people have to hire a stylist. Some people can coordinate clothing items and accessories into a very stylish ensemble. Some people can, and some people can't. Some people get very jealous of people with these natural stylish abilities.

Youtube this song: [City High ft. Eve – Caramel]

CHAPTER FIFTEEN:

Great Minds Talk About Ideas, Mediocre Minds Talk About Events, Small Minds Talk About People. Is That All the Gossip you got?

{Note: In this book, you will see many sentences, phrases, thoughts, and messages repeated several times. This is intentional. Because we are so thoroughly indoctrinated and saturated with the follower's way of thinking and the "old" way of doing things; ...new ideas, a new awareness and the process of transitioning philosophies, thoughts, and lifestyles requires a repetitive presentation.}

The people who gossip are (to some degree) insecure. The more insecure they are, the more they gossip. Most gossip is about negative topics. Insecure people gossip because they need to degrade someone else to make themselves feel better about themselves. It's a form of compare and compete and "EARNING EGO BONUS POINTS." They talk about other people having similar items, then compare what they have to the person they are talking about to see who has the "better" in the comparison.

Insecure individuals make up the largest portion of "FOLLOWERS" because they are insecure and never really confident enough to think independently. They follow the crowd because they are too lazy or incapable of formulating their own opinion. They always have to get someone else's opinion. They lack decision making/problem-solving skills.

They are never really sure of what they

should say, or what they should wear, or how they should behave. They are nervous and constantly questioning themselves.

This is related to GOSSIPING, in that the insecure, follower, gossiper tries to persuade others to talk badly about an individual. At first, you may think this is a leadership role {persuading others to believe as you do}, but what it really is, this insecure individual does not want to *stand alone* in their opinion.

A real LEADER is not afraid to stand alone, because they have the knowledge, intelligence, and analytical skills to develop an independent opinion supported by facts.

An INSECURE FOLLOWER - follows the crowd or wants to be ina crowd and tries to persuade others to go along with them sothey feel like they are within a crowd. "Misery loves Company."

The insecure follower takes compare and compete to the extreme. Gossiping is giving and getting information to perform the compare and compete. Gossiping is a way for the insecure follower to form alliances and friendships to join forces against the individuals of whom they are jealous.

This is especially true in the office/work environment. It is also quite prevalent in the church environment, as well.

A "friend," told me about one work situation where she and two coworkers had cubicles in a row. She said the coworkerson either side of her would listen to her phone conversations.The one in the cubicle to her right would call (on the office telephone) the one to her left and discuss her telephone conversations.

The stupid thing about this should be obvious. But since it wasn't apparent to them, maybe I need to explain it to you, as well. If they could hear her phone conversations, why wasn't it obvious to them that she could hear their conversations about her? At another job, this same friend experienced coworkers emailing nasty comments about her, back and forth.

So, I guess everybody knows that your coworkers smile in your face and talk about you behind your back.

I used to have a coworker who hated my guts, and I don't know why. I have my suspicions. She was so tightly wound up with hatred for me, we couldn't have a mature, civil conversation on the topic.

Whenever someone was gossiping and speaking badly about me, she was always ready to enthusiastically jump in, embellish, instigate, and add her hate-spewing comments.

In contrast, if someone would say something good about me, complimenting me, or spoke about my awards and accomplishments, she literally hissed, try to pivot, turn or stop the conversation, or she would simply ignore it or pretend she didn't hear any of the nice things said about me. People often have selective listening, selective comprehension, and selective memory. Selective listening: Some people hear what they want to hear. Some people twist the meaning of something they heard into what they want it to mean.

At orientation, a division leader stressed that "your reputation will precede you wherever you go. Try to maintain a good reputation." He stressed this, strongly and repeatedly.

This is good AND BAD advice.

I ascertained that gossiping was a very strong and supported part of this organization's corporate culture. It is terrible because it indirectly supports office gossip.

As a manager, I stress, "Approach each person on an individual basis. Give them a clean slate with which to start. Don't judge a person by rumors and reputation."

Just because one person had a GOOD experience with an individual, doesn't mean the next person will.

Just because one person had a BAD experience with an individual, doesn't mean the next person will.

You don't know who is at fault for the good or bad experience. There are always *at least* two sides to every story.

You can try really hard and work diligently to earn and maintain a good reputation, but some things are beyond your control, and you can never please all the people all the time.

People get in their office cliques and gossip groups and wallow and fester in negativity toward an individual. They spread this bad information with new employees, trying to recruit and strengthen the alliance against the outcast individual.

If you are a new team member, be very

careful about joining cliques and gossip groups. It is a very slippery slope and a double-edged sword.

Some people befriend you, get you to drop your guard, and get you to tell them your business so they can take it back to the gossip group or social clique.

Some people never graduate from the gossip, popular clique, immature mentality when they graduate from or drop out of high school. When I was a child, I talked like a child, I thought like a child, and reasoned like a child. When I became a man, I put childish ways behind me. 1 Corinthians 13:11

Some "WEAK, INSECURE, FOLLOWERS" practice degrading and diminishing others to make them feel better about themselves.

You have seen the insecure ones, always talking on the phone, always on social media. They are trying to gauge whether they fit into the "normal" and the popular trends. In other words, "following the crowd." They pay close attention to the feed-back to get a sense of agreement, approval, and validation. Got'ta get their "warm and fuzzies," can't stand alone in their opinion, can't stand to be alone, and can't stand silence.

Crabs in a Barrel: With the crabs in a barrel syndrome, the individual is "in essence" saying to others: "Stay stupid and dumb like me, so I won't feel so bad that I am stupid and dumb." "Don't try to achieve more than me, so I won't feel bad that I didn't achieve more." "Speak poorly and use improper grammar like me, so I won't feel bad that I don't know how to speak properly." "Don't think outside of the box, so I don't feel dumb and weak for not having the courage to think outside of the box." "Don't be an individual who is not a follower, so I won't be dazed and confused because I didn't realize that there was an option not to be a follower; therefore, I am stunned, and I don't know how to interact with a non-follower." "Don't speak intelligently or demonstrate your advanced intelligence so that I can feel superior to you."

The bad thing about gossip is that it spreads someone's personal information without their knowledge and consent. One of the worst elements of gossip is that the gossipers seldom get the subject's side of the story. Gossip gets embellished, stretched, twisted, spun and distorted as it passes from one person to the next. Sometimes the gossip is a completely fabricated, **a straight-up lie**, intended for harm and hurt.

People play the Gossip Game at parties where a sentence is whispered in the first person's ear in a long line of people. The sentence gets whispered consecutively from one person to the next, on down through the rest of the line.

At the end of the line, the last person says the sentence out loud to reveal that the sentence has been distorted or completely changed from the original sentence. This is how gossip occurs in real life. You can ruin someone's reputation, employment, and personal relationships with gossip.

Use your powers for good. It will come back to you.

YouTube this song: Timex Social Club –
Rumors Official Video

"Great minds talk about ideas. Mediocre minds talk about events. Small minds talk about people." Are 80% of your conversations degrading and belittling other people? Are most of your discussions talking behind someone's back about their personal and private business? Answer these questions HONESTLY. You may learn a little more about yourself.

The motive for gossiping CANNOT be to help, if the intention was to help, the information would be discussed with that individual and not discussed behind their backs and out of their presence. So, if the motive is NOT to help. So, what is the true motive?

www.ingramcontent.com/pod-product-compliance
Lightning Source LLC
La Vergne TN
LVHW051228080426
835513LV00016B/1480